D

JAMES JOYCE

Michael Murphy

Greenwich Exchange, London

First published in Great Britain in 2004
All rights reserved

James Joyce
© Michael Murphy 2004

Printed and bound by Q3 Digital/Litho, Loughborough
Tel: 01509 213456
Typesetting and layout by Albion Associates, London
Tel: 020 8852 4646
Cover design by December Publications, Belfast
Tel: 028 90286559

Cover: Photograph of James Joyce © Getty Images/Hulton Archive

Greenwich Exchange Website: www.greenex.co.uk

ISBN 1-871551-73-0

For John Lucas

Acknowledgements

I wish to express my gratitude to Dr Terry Philips and Liverpool Hope University College for the period of research leave during which I was able to complete this book. My thanks, too, to Alison Mark, Deryn Rees-Jones, Maurice Riordan and Matt Simpson for their helpful comments and suggestions.

Damn braces! Bless Relaxes!
William Blake

CONTENTS

Chronology

1882   James Augustine Joyce born 2nd February at 41 Brighton Square West, Rathgar, Dublin. The eldest child of John Stanislaus Joyce, a collector of rates, and Mary Jane ('May') Joyce (née Murray).

1883   John Stanislaus Joyce born 17th December.

1886   Gladstone's Home Rule Bill is defeated in the House of Commons.

1887   The Joyce family moves to an impressive house at 1 Martello Terrace in Bray, a seaside suburb south of Dublin. Joyce's uncle, William O'Connell, moves in with the family as does Mrs 'Dante' Hearn Conway, who acts as governess.

1888   In September Joyce sent to school at Clongowes Wood College in Co. Kildare. At six and a half he is the youngest boy at the school.

1889   Charles Stewart Parnell, MP, leader of the Irish Home Rule Party, is cited in divorce proceedings, accused of committing adultery with Katherine ('Kitty') O'Shea.

1890   Parnell is ousted as leader of the Home Rule Party.

1891   In June Joyce's father loses his job as rates collector for Dublin Corporation, a position he had held since 1882. He is forced to retire on a pension of just one-third of his salary. On 6th October Parnell dies in Brighton, England. Joyce's stay at Clongowes is abruptly cut short because of his family's worsening finances.

1893   Joyce is enrolled in the Christian Brothers School on North Richmond Street. In April Joyce and Stanislaus are offered a free education at Belvedere College, a Jesuit day-school on Great Denmark Street.

1895   Joyce elected a member of the Sodality of the Blessed Virgin, the aim of which is to instil high ideals plus Christian faith and morals in the schoolboys.

1896   Joyce elected Prefect of the Sodality, a position which makes him head boy in all but name.

1897   Joyce wins prize for best English composition for his age in Ireland.

1898   Joyce enrols in University College Dublin and studies Modern Languages.

1900   *The Fortnightly Review* publishes Joyce's review of Ibsen's *When We Dead Awake*. He receives a letter from Ibsen's English translator, William Archer, telling him that Ibsen thanks "Mr James Joyce" for his "very benevolent review". Joyce replies: "I am a young Irishman, 18 years old, and the words of Ibsen I shall keep in my heart all my life."

1901   After the college censor refuses to allow it to appear in the student paper, *St Stephen's*, Joyce publishes at his own expense a pamphlet called 'The Day of the Rabblement' which attacks the insularity of the Irish theatre.

1902   Joyce graduates from University College Dublin on 1st Devcember. With financial help from his father, George Russell ('A.E.'), W.B. Yeats and Lady Gregory, he leaves Dublin for Paris. After just two weeks in France, Joyce returns home for Christmas.

1903   In January Joyce returns to Paris. In March the Irish dramatist and poet John Millington Synge arrives in Paris. He finds Joyce "pretty badly off" and "wandering around Paris rather unbrushed and rather indolent". On 10th April Joyce receives a telegram from his father: "Mother dying come home Father." May Joyce dies of cancer on 13th August.

1904   On 7th January Joyce copies an essay entitled 'A Portrait of the Artist' into an exercise book belonging to his sister Mabel. On 10th June, Joyce meets the Galway-born Nora Barnacle. On 16th June Joyce and Nora meet again for their first date. On 14th September Joyce leaves the Martello tower at

Sandycove where he has been living with the hard-drinking, Oxford-educated, medical student and poet, Oliver St John Gogarty, after Gogarty fires a revolver at some pots and pans hanging over Joyce's bed. Joyce has three stories published by George Russell in *The Irish Homestead*: 'The Sisters' (August), 'Eveline' (September) and 'After the Race' (December). Joyce begins work on an autobiographical novel, *Stephen Hero*. On 8th October Joyce and Nora sail from Dublin's North Wall, and arrive in Trieste on 20th October. There is no work for Joyce in Trieste, and the couple travel to Pola, a military port on the Istrian coast. In December, Nora discovers that she is pregnant.

1905   In March Joyce and Nora move to Trieste, where Joyce begins teaching at the Berlitz school. Birth of Giorgio Joyce on 29th July. In October, following a request for help from Joyce, Stanislaus arrives from Dublin.

1906   Consisting at this point of 12 stories, *Dubliners* is dispatched for publication to Grant Richards in London. Joyce, Nora and Giorgio arrive in Rome on 31st July, where Joyce has secured a job working in a bank. Joyce begins writing 'The Dead'.

1907   In March Joyce is robbed and then arrested in a street brawl in Rome. *Chamber Music*, a collection of 36 poems written mostly between 1901-4, published by Elkin Mathews in May. In July Joyce contracts rheumatic fever after a drinking bout that leaves him unconscious in a gutter. Joyce is hospitalised, and contracts the first of a series of painful and debilitating eye conditions. Birth of Lucia Joyce on 25th July. Finishes 'The Dead' in September and begins re-writing the 26 chapters of *Stephen Hero* as *A Portrait of the Artist as a Young Man*.

1908   Joyce completes first three chapters of *A Portrait*, and then sets them aside because of family tensions. On 4th August Nora suffers a miscarriage three months into pregnancy.

1909   In July and August Joyce visits Dublin with Giorgio, hoping to secure a contract with Maunsel & Co. for the publication of the revised version of *Dubliners*. A draft contract is agreed, stating that the book will appear in print by March 1910. Joyce signs a contract with three Triestine businessmen in October for the establishment of the first public cinema in Dublin. The *Volta* opens its doors on 20th December.

1910   In January Joyce returns to Trieste. The *Volta* fails, and is sold at a loss of £600. Publication of *Dubliners* is delayed. Joyce begins selling suits, homespuns and tweeds from the Dublin Woollen Company to his Triestine acquaintants.

1911   Maunsel & Co. defer publication of *Dubliners*, demanding a number of cuts and alterations. Solicitors advise them that the inclusion of the names of living persons in the text may be libellous. Home Rule is passed in the House of Commons, only to be defeated in the House of Lords.

1912   In August and September Joyce visits Ireland for what will prove the last time. Negotiations with Maunsel & Co. finally collapse, and all but one set of the proofs of *Dubliners* are destroyed. In retaliation, Joyce writes 'Gas from a Burner' ("Ladies and gents, you are here assembled/To hear why earth and heaven trembled/Because of the black and sinister arts/Of an Irish writer in foreign parts.") and has it published on his return to Trieste.

1913   In November Joyce makes one last effort to publish *Dubliners*, contacting Grant Richards again. Richards agrees to re-read the manuscript. Joyce is approached by Ezra Pound, who has heard of him from Yeats.

1914   Joyce sends Pound a copy of *Dubliners* and a revised version of the opening chapter of *A Portrait*. Pound asks to publish a poem ('I hear an Army') in an Imagist anthology in the USA, and begins serialising *A Portrait* in 15-page instalments in the *Egoist*. Publication assured, Joyce hurries to complete the last two chapters. On 15th June Grant Richards publishes 1,250 copies of *Dubliners*. Outbreak of the First World War. In November Joyce writes notes for a play, *Exiles*. Begins *Ulysses*.

1915   Stanislaus is interned in an Austrian detention centre on 9th January, where he remains for the rest of the war. *Exiles* completed. Joyce writes to Stanislaus on 16th June that "the first episode of my new novel *Ulysses* is written". Joyce, Nora and the children leave Trieste for neutral Zurich on 27th June. *Dubliners* sells just 33 copies in a year.

1916   Easter Uprising on 24th April in Dublin. *Dubliners* and *A Portrait* published by B.W. Huebsch in New York. Joyce writes 'A Notebook of Dreams', a record of his wife's dreams alongside his own interpretations.

1917   English edition of *A Portrait* published in February by Egoist Press. Harriet Shaw Weaver, editor of the *Egoist*, begins making anonymous donations into Joyce's bank account which will continue for the rest of Joyce's life. Weaver signs a contract to publish *Ulysses* serially in the *Egoist*. Joyce suffers a fierce attack of glaucoma and undergoes an iridectomy.

1918   Along with an English actor, Claud W. Sykes, Joyce co-founds The English Players Theatre Company and mounts a production of Wilde's *The Importance of Being Earnest*. The company follows this with a triple bill that includes Synge's *Riders to the Sea*, with Nora playing Cathleen. The serial publication of *Ulysses* begins in the *Little Review* in March. *Exiles* is published in May by Grant Richards. The Armistice is signed on 11th November.

1919   Irish War of Independence begins in January. The January and March issues of the *Little Review* containing chapters from *Ulysses* are confiscated and burned by the US Postal Authorities. In Britain, the *Egoist* publishes edited versions of four episodes from *Ulysses*. In August the first production of *Exiles* receives poor notices in Munich. Joyce returns in October with his family to Trieste.

1920   In June Joyce and Pound meet for the first time. Pound encourages him to move to Paris. The January and July-August issues of *Little Review* are again confiscated by the US Postal Authorities.

1921   Convicted and fined for publishing obscenity, the editors of the *Little Review* cease serialising *Ulysses*. Sylvia Beach, the American founder of the Shakespeare and Company bookshop in Paris, offers to publish the novel – the edition to be funded in advance by subscription. In October Joyce completes 'Ithaca', the last episode of *Ulysses* to be drafted. In December the treaty granting southern Ireland dominion status is signed.

1922   In February the first two published copies of *Ulysses* are delivered to Joyce in time for his 40th birthday. Irish Civil war breaks out. In April Nora and the children are visiting Ireland when their train is fired upon by troops.

1923   Despite the reoccurrence of his eye troubles, in March Joyce begins work on *Work in Progress* (later *Finnegans Wake)*. In May the Irish Civil War ends, and the Irish Free State joins the League of Nations.

1924   Extracts from *Work in Progress* published in *Transatlantic Review* in April.

1925   First English production of *Exiles* is produced at the Neighbourhood Playhouse in New York.

1927   Shakespeare and Company publish *Pomes Penyeach* in July.

1928   Joyce meets Samuel Beckett.

1929   A dozen writers, including Beckett, Frank Budgen, Stuart Gilbert and William Carlos Williams collectively produce *Our Exagmination Round His Factification for Incamination of Work in Progress*, a guide to, and apologia for, the as-yet-unfinished *Finnegans Wake*. Also included are two hostile "letters of protest".

1930   The first critical study of *Ulysses* is published: *James Joyce's 'Ulysses'* by Stuart Gilbert.

1931   Nora and Joyce marry in London on 4th July so as to secure Giorgio and Lucia's inheritance. John Joyce dies on 29th December.

1932   In February Stephen James Joyce is born to Giorgio and Helen Joyce. Lucia suffers the first in a series of breakdowns, and enters a clinic.

1933   Lucia hospitalised in Nyon near Zurich. In December an American judge delivers the opinion that *Ulysses* is not obscene and can be published in the USA.

1934   US edition of *Ulysses* published by Random House. Lucia is now under the care of Carl Jung.

1936   *Ulysses* published in London by Bodley Head. *Collected Poems* published in New York.

1938   In January Samuel Beckett is stabbed in a Paris street by a pimp to whom he refuses to give money. Joyce has him moved to a private room at his own expense, and lends him a reading lamp. Joyce finishes *Finnegans Wake* on 13th November.

1939   On 18th January W.B. Yeats dies in the south of France. *Finnegans Wake* is published in London and New York on 4th May. On 1st September Germany invades Poland. France and Britain declare war on Germany on 3rd September. The Joyce family leave Paris for Vichy.

1940   On 17th June France falls to the Nazis. The French Senate and the Chamber of Deputies meet at Vichy on 10th July and vote full powers to govern the country and draft a new constitution to Marshall Pétain.

1941   Joyce dies alone at 2.15 in the morning of 13th January after surgery on a perforated ulcer. Two days later he is buried in Zurich's Fluntern cemetery, without the last rites of the Catholic Church.

1951   Nora Joyce dies in Zurich on 10th April and is buried in the same cemetery but in a separate grave from Joyce. The priest who presides over her funeral describes her as "eine grosse Sünderin" ("a great sinner").

1955   Stanislaus Joyce dies in Trieste.

1966   On 16th June the remains of Joyce and Nora are moved from their separate graves to a permanent plot. At the graveside a sculpture by Milton Hebald shows Joyce sitting crosslegged, smoking a cigarette.

Introduction

In comparison to other writers – Joseph Conrad, say, or Ernest Hemingway, men who, as Joyce enviously said about Hemingway, were ready to live the lives they wrote about – Joyce's was a strikingly uneventful life. After school he went to University, followed by a brief fling with Bohemian Paris and life as a medical student. Back in Ireland he hitched up with the first woman to reciprocate his feelings. They moved abroad, had two children – one of each, as they say – and over the course of four decades he produced two volumes of poetry, a play, three novels and a book of short stories. Such, at least, are the superficial facts. In actuality Joyce's was as daring and provocative a life as any he might have aspired to. It's just that with Joyce, as with his fiction, the devil is in the detail. Every lived experience was subject to its fictional re-presentation, even to the point of his manufacturing or stage-managing certain events so that he might the more accurately write about them. Though the differences between them were often profound, Joyce would have agreed with Yeats that the writer faced but two options: perfection of the life or art.

This is not to say that Joyce had an easy time of it. Though he was born into a comfortable Dublin middle-class Catholic family, Joyce discovered the vicissitudes of material life early. As is told in his first completed novel, the beguilingly autobiographical *A Portrait of the Artist as a Young Man* (1916), the Joyce family moved house five times in a dozen years – each move, as though paralleling the circles of Dante's Inferno, spiralling ever nearer to Dublin's cripplingly impoverished inner city that lay stewing northside of the river Liffey. Poverty was to be a constant theme of Joyce's life. Indeed, it wasn't until the last decade of his life that publication of *Ulysses* (1922) and sections of the novel that was to become *Finnegans Wake* (1939) saw him and his family financially secure. By then, however, he was all but blind after recurrent eye problems and his daughter Lucia was being treated for a series of mental breakdowns. In between times, he lived in a succession of cities – Paris, Pola, Trieste, Rome and Zurich – the decision to move often being decided by the pressing events of two world wars. Even in death he wasn't guaranteed any secure resting-place. In 1966 his grave was opened so that he could be reunited with the body of his wife, Nora.

Hardly surprising, then, that most of the major incidents in Joyce's writing are to do with journeys: from his early school essay on the Greek mythological hero Ulysses, to the perambulations of various characters through the Dublin of *Dubliners*; from Stephen Dedalus' journey to Cork with his father, to the bar of soap that takes up occupancy in various pockets of Bloom's clothing in *Ulysses*. His only play, *Exiles*, is about a writer returned from abroad to an Ireland that proves unwelcoming; and *Finnegans Wake*, with its circular structure – the first and last sentences are joined like a snake biting its own tail – mirrors the constant restless urgency of a man who, in Seamus Deane's words, saw walking as a focus for "conversation, flashbacks, meditations".

What Joyce set in motion there has been no shortage of critical commentary eager to keep moving. For the reader setting out on the great enterprise of reading Joyce there is a bewildering array of scholarly material currently available, a great deal of which comes close to Buck Mulligan's description in *Ulysses* of an imaginary book on Irish mythology: "five lines of text and ten pages of notes". The best of these are invaluable to the general reader and student of literature alike. Their main worth (one that might prove a rough guide to any writing on Joyce), is that they help to make the discovery of his work one of the great pleasures of a lifetime of reading. As with a guidebook to a favourite city, they should repay repeated reading, nudging one's shoulder at a particular view from a bridge, making suggestions about the best restaurants, pointing out a beautiful still-life in a corner of a museum. Others are frankly less helpful. To risk a generalisation, these can be spotted fairly easily and usually have titles which mimic the language of *Finnegans Wake*. This isn't to entirely dismiss such books. In America especially they are a cottage industry and help keep a fair number of families fed and stabled. But while there's always something to be said for the crooked path leading to the palace of wisdom, the problem with this kind of approach is that it can divert the reader into a labyrinth of Joycean arcana, distracting them from the main task of reading Joyce rather than his scholastic acolytes.

For this state of affairs Joyce is himself not unblameworthy. Asked why *Ulysses* was written in the way it was, he replied: "To keep the critics busy for three hundred years." The note of evasion is important, as is the possibility that Joyce was looking for a less abrasive way of saying 'Read it, and see for yourself!' Joyce's writings can be approached without the literary equivalent of a team of sherpas, though the reader who wanders alone through the foothills of *Dubliners* or *A Portrait of the Artist as a Young Man* will want some assistance with the later novels. For while it simply isn't true that *Ulysses* is incomprehensible without a secondary guide, it goes without saying that any good guide will lead the reader into aspects of the novel that might otherwise have remained hidden. And anyway, difficulty, uncertainty and doubt are part of human experience and must therefore play a part in the novel, that most accommodating of literary forms. *Finnegans Wake*, however, is something of a law unto itself. While recognising that it is in its own eccentric and imposing way an organic development of vital aspects of Joyce's thinking about history, fiction and language, there are problems with it that aren't easily dealt with and which come close to Joyce's comment that "The demand that I make of my reader is that he should devote his whole life to reading my works." Such a reader might indeed find that *Finnegans Wake* re-paid this monkish devotion; for the rest of us, the Joyce of *Ulysses* in particular is a writer alongside other moderns such as Kafka, Proust, Mann, Borges and Calvino the slightest familiarity with whom sends us back to our lives with a renewed sense of the remarkable capacity human beings have for building themselves a home in language.

Even at his most naked and vulnerable, Edgar in *King Lear* has language as a refuge: "I Edgar nothing am". In saying so he breaks apart and dismantles the grammatical and syntactical laws of language, re-defining himself and the world through an act of verbal estrangement which, though it expresses his terror at his own tragic circumstances, can also be seen as the very moment in the play when, through language, he asserts his own individual self and destiny.

Ironically, it is only having fallen so far that Edgar discovers the power within himself to overcome the vertigo of history. Such is the use to which Joyce puts language. Increasingly in his writings it is used not to reflect or comment on the world, but rather to radically re-define and re-fashion it and thus celebrate it in all its stubborn grace and fortitude. Why he should feel so acutely the need to do so is considered in the next chapter.

1

Those Big Words: Joyce and Ireland

Every great work of literature redefines our strategies for reading. As the French writer Roland Barthes provocatively wrote:

> All modes of writing have in common the fact of being 'closed' and thus different from spoken language. Writing is in no way an instrument of communication, it is not an open route through which there passes only the intention to speak.[1]

I will return to Barthes later. For now it is worth glossing his words by saying that the experience of attempting to read such a text as Barthes describes is a rediscovery of the possibilities of language as something other than, in Barthes' words, "the intention to speak." This is not to say that literary greatness can be measured in terms of difficulty or obscurity; simply that the merit of such a book, as with Edgar's all-too-vivid realisation of the essential vulnerability of the human condition, is that it forces us to ask questions of ourselves and our expectations of what it is to use words. This is as true for *Don Quixote* as it is for *Ulysses*, *Middlemarch* or *Midnight's Children*. Speech, Barthes says, is epitomised by its expendability. Writing, on the other hand, "is always rooted in something beyond language, it develops like a seed, not like a line, it manifests an essence and holds the threat of a secret ... it is intimidating." The precise nature of this act of resistance or intimidation will always be aesthetic. That is, it will manifest itself as a work of art, the text operating as a border crossing between our necessarily limited knowledge of the world and the limitless possibilities of its fictional representation. We need only think, for example, of the differences between a portrait of a woman by Piero della Francesca and one by Lucian Freud, or the fact that Joyce called his first novel *A Portrait* (suggesting that it is only one of a possible many) *of the Artist* (single, definitive, archetypal). The sources from which this aesthetic sense springs are many and varied. And though saying what this source is may be relatively simple, putting it into writing – into art – can be infinitely difficult.

In Joyce's case this "something beyond language" is the historical fact of Empire – the British Empire which governed Ireland politically, and the Holy Roman Empire whose dominance was both spiritual and economic. Put simply, everything he wrote, from his earliest poem, 'Et Tu, Healy', composed when he was just nine years-old, to the closing pages of *Finnegans Wake* are written in defiance of what, in an article called 'The Home Rule Comet', he defined as "The fogginess that usually envelopes the shores of Britain thickened so as to shroud them in a dense and impenetrable cloudiness." Such meteorological references abound in Joyce's writings. We need only think of the overcast skies that loom over a number of the stories in *Dubliners*, threaten to drown Dublin in a deluge of Biblical proportions in *A Portrait of the Artist as a Young Man*, and at the beginning of *Finnegans Wake* result in the enormous thunderclap that signals the Fall.

In wider critical terms, these lowering skies can be thought of as functioning in a way analogous to ideology, or what Michel Foucault termed "the different modes by which in our culture, human beings are made subjects". Put simply, ideology is how political, cultural, economic or religious power is defined, defended and implemented. For example, the British Empire was premised, in part at least, by the notion that it was the 'white man's burden' to civilise 'backward' nations. Similarly, Germany's expansion under Hitler was based on a belief in the inherent superiority of German culture. And after the terrorist attacks of 11th September 2001 the US threatened, in the words of a CIA officer, "to export death and violence to the four corners of the earth" in defence of America and American interests. These are extreme examples, and I hope the reader will bear with me for referring to them here. That I do so, however, is simply to locate Joyce in an Ireland and a Dublin very different from the thriving, self-confident 'Celtic Tiger' of the early 21st century – a country which, though it retains vestiges of religious, sexual and racial intolerance, and remains very much a bastion of one of the two

Empires Joyce railed against – Rome – has fought free at least of British hegemony. Returning to the Ireland of Joyce's youth and early manhood, however, we can see that the Irish people were subjects of a British monarch and a British Parliament. There were obvious manifestations of this: soldiers on the streets and at railway stations, Imperial red pillar boxes and recruiting posters for the British army in the post offices. All this Joyce records. What he also records are the ways in which ideology imposes itself not simply through consciousness but through the representation and practices of everyday life. Such systems and structures as they appear in language are called discourse; and it is through discourse that the individual comes to accept the representation of themselves as proposed by such authorities as the Church, the family, the media and literature. Susan Sontag has discussed these things in relation to photography and American culture, saying how ideology comes along with an entourage of "poster-ready images", the "visual equivalent of sound bites". Ideology, she argues, is a component of "what a society chooses to think about."[2] Joyce understood this and made it the stuff of his fiction. He also went further, looking not only at *what* we think but *how* we think. In the 'Nausicaa' episode of *Ulysses*, for example, he shows how the portrayal of women in the discourses of religion, popular fiction, fashion magazines and fairy tale construct images of femininity that limit and hinder not only the ways in which women act and think about themselves but how men act towards and think about women.

The simple fact is that Joyce's writings are radical because they are political. To ignore this or to paper-over the facts as Steven Connor does in his guide to Joyce is to miss the point. When, for example, Connor says that "*Ulysses* is ... a didactic work, whose aim is the education of the reader, *though that education has no moral or political aim*" [my italics] we can only wonder what Connor understands by education if, in the fullest possible sense, it isn't both moral and political. Without these things in place it seems to me highly unlikely that the postmodern reader imagined by Connor would bother with Joyce's writings in the first place, or what they would have to gain from doing so. Let us be clear then: Joyce's politics are aimed at those institutions and forms of discourse that he saw as oppressing Ireland and the Irish people. Among these were representations of the Irish in literature. As William Carlos Williams said in an article defending Joyce against Rebecca West's criticism of *Ulysses*, Joyce cannot be taken "into the body of English literature for fear of the destructive forces of such an act ... Joyce has broken through ... a fact English criticism cannot tolerate." That it took an American to recognise that Joyce was "cutting all England away from under" West's argument shouldn't surprise us; likewise, that Joyce's great achievement lay in throwing off the winding clothes of Empire by rejecting those forms of language used to maintain it:

> Meanings are perverted by time and chance – but kept perverted by academic observance and intention. At worst they are inactive and get only the static value of anything, which retains its shape but is dead. All words, all sense of being gone out of them. Or trained into them by the dull of the deadly minded. Joyce is restoring them. ... Joyce has not changed his words beyond recognition. They remain to the quick eye the same. But many of the stultifying associations of the brutalized mind (brutalized by modern futility) have been lost in his process.[3]

This is as clear an analysis of the workings of ideology and Joyce's Herculean task of undermining it as we could want.

I will be returning to Joyce's engagement with ideology throughout what follows. For now, though, I want to outline a little of the history of Ireland's relationship with the British mainland. Only when armed with an understanding of the centuries-old complexities of Anglo-Irish relations can we begin to fully recognise that Joyce's aesthetic structures are both a response to, and an attempt at re-writing, this history.

Though fascinated by them, Joyce came to distrust all myths that determined a moment of irretrievable catastrophe, a Fall from grace after which humanity was damned. Whether the Fall of Adam and Eve in the Garden of Eden, or the loss of Ireland's 'uncrowned King' in Parnell's ignominious downfall, he saw such myths as giving lie to the fact that there had been a time when human identity was fixed and singular. Such a belief, Joyce understood, limited the individual and state alike. For while in our daily lives we are bedevilled by our First Parents' decision to eat of the Tree of Knowledge, so in the political life of Ireland there existed competing claims to representing the true Ireland, an essential Irishness untouched by centuries of conflict and colonialism. Cutting a path through these thickets of claim and counter claim was, Joyce knew, futile. If, for argument's sake, we date 1541 as the downfall of a fully independent Ireland – the year that Henry VIII assumed the title 'King of Ireland' – we are left with the problem that Ireland had, since the conquests of the 12th century, been a 'lordship' of the English Crown. And while Henry's assumption of the title can be regarded as a clear indication of his commitment to absolute rule, it overlooks the fact that his willingness to do so arose not solely from English ambition but came at the prompting of the Irish Council, the hope being that allegiance to a single figure of authority would undermine Ireland's competing local allegiances.

Even in the early 17th century the Crown's ability to govern Ireland was at best patchy. Then, as now, Ireland was characterised by a fragmented and fractious sense of identity: what was meant by 'Irishness' was as changeable as the weather in Mayo. And if the country's political and cultural identity remained fluid, so too did knowledge of the land. Many areas remained unmapped, and surveyors looking to fill in the blanks did so in the face of physical intimidation. In short, the English were unable to map and plot the landscape, and as a result they were unable to 'read' Ireland. And where maps or verbal descriptions existed, they were often inaccurate; the difficulties of the terrain being exaggerated because the observer was seeing things from a military perspective. Thus a small wood became a large wood, because it was no longer trees that defined the area but its capacity to harbour rebel militia. Over time, of course, the resulting maps and plots became palimpsests of a conquering army's fears and anxieties. Little wonder that by the time of Cromwell's arrival in 1649, his army were minded to prosecute a 'shoot to kill' policy. As the massacres of civilian populations at Drogheda and Wexford demonstrated, little distinction was made between actual rebels and the rest of the Irish population.

Changes in England's political fortune and direction continued to be felt in Ireland. Under the Catholic monarch James II, Irish Roman Catholics were advanced to positions of state and placed in control of the militia. As a consequence, the Roman Catholic population sided with James II in the English Revolution of 1688. Thus, in 1689, when James landed at Dublin with his French officers, an Irish army was ready to assist him. Protestant settlers were driven from their homes and found refuge in the towns of Enniskillen and Londonderry, which James attempted to capture. He was hampered by his lack of artillery and the city was relieved by way of the sea. Nevertheless, in 1689 his Parliament restored all lands confiscated since 1641 and passed an act of attainder against the partisans of King William III. In the following year, however, William landed in Ireland and, in July 1690, defeated the Irish forces in the Battle of the Boyne. It is in celebration of this victory that Protestants in Northern Ireland and in cities such as Liverpool and Glasgow still march today.

Throughout this period the English crushed Irish commerce and industries: successive enactments in 1665 and 1680 banned the Irish export trade to England in cattle, milk, butter, and cheese; and in 1699 the trade in woollens, which had grown up among the Irish Protestants, was likewise halted. (On this point, it is useful to bear in mind that Ireland's trading links with mainland Britain are a recurrent motif in *Ulysses*.) The result of these measures was gradual economic decline. Many Irish emigrated from the country – Catholics to Spain and France, Protestants to America.

The world of 18th-century Ireland arouses strong and, more often than not, contradictory emotions. To Yeats it was "that one Irish century that escaped from darkness and confusion", while to the Dublin-born, English-educated novelist Elizabeth Bowen it conjured images of "great bold rooms, the high doors impos[ing] an order on life. Sun blazed in at the windows, fires roared in the grate. ... Life still kept a touch of colonial vigour; at the same time ... it was bound up in the quality of a dream." As the historian R.F. Foster has said, however, belief in such a dream "required a personal commitment to the history of the Ascendancy class", one that would not be shared by Catholics or those of Dissenting traditions. To the Belfast-born poet Louis MacNeice, Foster adds, the Ascendancy was "Nothing but an insidious bonhomie, an obsolete bravado and a way with

horses."[4]

The century ended with a perennial fact of Irish life and a major theme of Joyce's fiction: betrayal. Given assurances by the British Prime Minister, William Pitt the Younger, that if they supported the Act of Union Ireland's Catholics would receive emancipation, the Catholic hierarchy helped suppress the rebellion of 1798. The Act of Union was subsequently ratified by both the British and Irish Parliaments on 1st January 1801 and effectively abolished the Irish Parliament. Dublin, though it remained the capital, no longer exercised any legislative authority. What is more, owing to the opposition of George III, Pitt was unable to make good his promises. For the majority in Ireland the situation was simple, and best summed up in the words of Jonathan Swift: "government without the consent of the governed is the very definition of slavery."

In many ways Swift's acerbic comment brings us close to the state of Ireland at the time of Joyce's birth in 1882, and to those events which most closely tie Joyce's early life with the political turmoil of his homeland and which for the Joyce family as well as the nation as a whole came to assume the ineluctable authority of myth.

In May 1882, the imprisoned Charles Stewart Parnell was set free from Dublin's Kilmainham Jail after serving six months for his membership of the outlawed Land League. The greatest political leader of nationalist Ireland since Daniel O'Connell almost half a century earlier, Parnell figures strongly in the imagination of Ireland and Irishness. Indeed, it is hardly overstating the case to say that if Parnell had not existed – his aristocratic personality, his spectacular fall from power following the exposure of his ten-year adulterous relationship with Katherine O'Shea, his subsequent 'betrayal' by Gladstone, the Catholic hierarchy, Ireland's rural population, and ultimately his own Irish Parliamentary Party – then Joyce would have had to invent him. He stands as a defining figure, almost an alter ego, for Joyce and for Stephen Dedalus who assesses the relationship between the individual and Ireland and Irish history thus:

> No honourable and sincere man … has given up to you his life and his youth and his affections from the days of Tone to those of Parnell but you sold him to the enemy or failed him in need or reviled him and left him for another. And you invite

7

me to be one of them. ... You talk to me of nationality, language, religion. I shall try to fly by those nets. [p. 220. See note on editions on p. 114].

Parnell's downfall had catastrophic repercussions for Irish society and culture. And though R.F. Foster for one discounts the idea that the 25 years between Parnell's death in Brighton in 1891 and the Easter Rising of April 1916 created a vacuum in Irish politics, Joyce's own reading of the situation, as evidenced by his story 'Ivy Day in the Committee Room', is that such a vacuum did exist and gave rise to political, intellectual and creative torpor. Set on the anniversary of Parnell's death (the title refers to the fact that at Parnell's funeral the mourners wore leaves in their lapels plucked from the ivy plants growing in Glasnevin Cemetery), the story highlights the petty rivalries and corruption of Dublin politics – a politics which was all but powerless to effect real change in Ireland, and which remained in hock to the British Empire. The story ends with Joe Hynes reciting a poem, 'The Death of Parnell', in which Parnell appears as "Our Uncrowned King" and Ireland is personified as "Erin, mourn[ing] with grief and woe". As a piece of soap-box sentiment, the poem works fine. Indeed, Hynes' *in memoriam* isn't dissimilar to the surviving fragment of Joyce's own poem in tribute to Parnell, 'Et Tu, Healy'.[5] The fact remains, however, that Joyce was just nine-years-old and, we imagine, parroting the sentiments of his father and family friends in his eulogy.

Where Foster and Joyce agree is that the quarter of a century preceding the Easter Uprising did bring about a clash of generations that Foster describes as "Fathers of the old parliamentary era were confronted by Sons (and Daughters) who were affected by other, less compromising commitments." Joyce, for one, found compromise of whatever kind anathema. All of his fiction can be read as an attempt at trying to resolve the conflicts that exist between fathers and their offspring, between external forms of authority and self-governance, and which as late as 1934, in 'Epilogue to Ibsen's *Ghosts*', a play which examines the effects on a son of inheriting his father's syphilis, he characterised as:

Silenced and smothered by my past
Like the lewd knight in dirty linen

I struggle forth to swell the cast
And air a long-suppressed opinion.

That the father rather than the son speaks the poem only adds to the sense that Joyce, himself by now a parent, was never fully able to bridge the 'generation gap'. To the end of his life he kept with him a portrait of John Joyce, and in 'Ecce Puer' (1932) the death of this father and the birth of a first grandchild become fused in the one event:

A child is sleeping:
An old man gone.
O, father forsaken,
Forgive your son!

It would hardly be reading too much into the poem to see it as expressing a desire to atone for more wide-ranging griefs and betrayals.

Before leaving Irish history for Joyce's steadily ever more fantastic re-imagining of it, I want briefly to say something about the portrayal of Ireland and the Irish that dominated the British media towards the end of the 19th century.

While the Elizabethans found the native Irish 'mere' in the sense of 'pure', such a word gradually came to denote inferiority and barbarism. It is in such terms that much of the London-based press continued to describe the Irish. At times this resulted in the crudest attempts at character assassination, as when letters published in the *Times* tried to link Parnell to the Phoenix Park murders of 1882. Other commentaries looked to dehumanise the Irish completely. Take this from the author and Anglican priest, Charles Kingsley, who, during a visit to Sligo in 1860, wrote about the Irish in such a way as to degrade both them and all black races:

I am haunted by the human chimpanzees I saw along that hundred miles of open country. [T]o see white chimpanzees is dreadful; if they were black, one would not feel it so much,

but their skins, except where tanned by exposure, are as white
as ours.

Little wonder, then, that more than a century later the characters of
Roddy Doyle's novel *The Commitments* continue to refer to the Irish
as "The niggers of Europe".

Elsewhere the effect was more insidious. For example, in *On the
Study of Celtic Literature* (1867), Matthew Arnold focused on the
concepts of 'race' and 'blood' in defining Ireland's national 'style';
concepts which, by focusing on an identifiable set of physical,
linguistic and spiritual characteristics, ignored, as Lionel Trilling
was later to comment, "all other determinants such as class, existing
social forms, and geographical and economic environment". For
Arnold, the Celt is sentimental and lively, yet lacking in patience
and self-control; essentially feminine, they are close to "natural
magic", prone to "extravagance and exaggeration"; ineffectual in
politics, they are "always ready to react against the despotism of
fact". Joyce for one had his own revenge on Arnold and his ambition
to Hellenise (i.e. civilise) Western culture. Twice he makes an
appearance in *Ulysses*: firstly as "A deaf gardener, aproned, masked
with Matthew Arnold's face" who witnesses the de-bagging of an
Oxford undergraduate; and then again in 'Circe', this time as "two
Oxford dons with lawnmowers ... masked with Matthew Arnold's
face". It is this aspect of Anglo-Irish relations that Buck Mulligan
represents in *Ulysses*. The point Joyce is making, then, is that Arnold's
Hellenism was in itself a decoy for British hegemony, one of the
bastions of which was Oxford University (or "Oxenford" as Joyce
renamed it). And as he makes clear in his essay on Oscar Wilde,
Joyce regarded Arnold's Hellenism as 'masking' or suppressing other
aspects of behaviour:

> [T]he truth is that Wilde, far from being a monster of perversion
> that inexplicably arose in the midst of the modern civilisation
> of England, is the logical and inevitable product of the Anglo-
> Saxon college and university system, a system of seclusion
> and secrecy.

What this "seclusion and secrecy" leads to, in Joyce's analysis, are
acts of subjugated violence and male rape. Wilde's 'crime', then,

was not so much sexual as social: "His greatest crime was to have caused in England a scandal".

Arnold's ideas can be seen as harmless, on a par with the scores of Irish jokes still doing the rounds today. Read in the context of other 19th-century representations of Ireland and the Irish, however, they can be seen as contributing to an armada of prejudices that saw Irish emigrants in London accused of everything from blacklegging, strike-breaking and undercutting the wages of labourers, to being carriers of typhus – commonly known as 'Irish fever'. They were generally characterised as rowdy, drunk and violent; and, following ethnological 'research' that linked the Celtic cranium to apes, would have seen themselves caricatured in *Punch* by John Tenniel, the illustrator of Lewis Carroll's *Alice* books, as either ape-like or, in his response to the killing of two English emissaries in Dublin's Phoenix Park, *The Irish Frankenstein*, as "Hideous, blood-stained, bestial, ruthless in its rage, implacable in its revengefulness, cynical in its contemptuous challenge of any authority". At one point *Punch* even described the working-class Irish as "the missing link between the gorilla and the Negro".

It is in this context, then, that we are best approaching the character studies that make up Joyce's *Dubliners*. For though there is no doubt that taken together the stories (described by Joyce as a "polished looking glass" in which the Irish people could have "one good look at themselves") caused offence, Joyce meant them as an antidote both to the British view of Ireland and, equally important, Ireland's collusion in that process of self-deception. They are stories which take us beyond the hackneyed image of the stage Irishman with his gift of the gab and her blarney, and tune in on frequencies of silence and denial.

Footnotes

[1] From 'Writing Degree Zero' in *A Roland Barthes Reader*, edited by Susan Sontag (Vintage: London, 1993).

[2] *Regarding the Pain of Others*, Susan Sontag (London: Hamish Hamilton, 2003).

[3] 'A Point for American Criticism' (1929), *Selected Essays of William Carlos Williams* (New York: New Directions, 1969), pp. 80-90.

[4] *Modern Ireland: 1600-1972* (Penguin: London, 1988).

[5] Timothy Michael Healy was Parnell's secretary in America in 1880, and MP for various Irish constituencies in the years between 1880-1910. After Parnell's death he became co-leader of the anti-Parnellite Irish National Federation. In 1922 he was made the first Governor-General of the Irish Free State.

2

Most Malicious Kind: *Dubliners*

Joyce began writing the stories that were to be collected as *Dubliners* when he was just 22 years old. The first story to be completed, 'The Sisters', was written at the instigation of George Russell, to whom Joyce had sent a 102-page chapter of *Stephen Hero*, the autobiographical novel that was later to be scrapped by Joyce and radically re-cast as *A Portrait of the Artist as a Young Man*. Russell read and admired what Joyce sent him, and in July 1904 asked if he would write a short story suitable for publication in the *Irish Homestead*. "It is easily earned money," Russell added, "if you can write fluently and don't mind playing to the common understanding and liking for once in a way." Joyce could write fluently. That he was prepared to patronise Russell's idea of the "common understanding" is another matter.

The nature of Joyce's departure from the prescription given him by Russell is immediately apparent. Later extensively rewritten, 'The Sisters' tells of the death of an old, paralysed and conscious-stricken priest from the point of view of a young boy whom the priest has been 'grooming' for the priesthood. The story is full of disquieting silences and omissions: "I wouldn't like children of mine ... to have too much to say to a man like that," says one character about the relationship between the boy and the priest. And while there is no evidence that the boy has suffered physical abuse at the hands of the priest (though Old Cotter's hints and whispers tend to leave us with the impression that, to his mind at least, the priest is homosexual), the portrait of the priest presented by the narrator remains deeply unsettling:

> Sometimes he used to put me through the responses of the
> Mass which he had made me learn by heart; and, as I pattered,

he used to smile pensively and nod his head, now and then pushing huge pinches of snuff up each nostril alternatively. When he smiled he used to uncover his big discoloured teeth and let his tongue lie upon his lower lip – a habit which made me feel uneasy in the beginning of our acquaintance before I knew him well. [p. 5]

While I'd want to counter the argument that Joyce's treatment of the priest is homophobic, it is certainly disquieting to see homosexuality being used as a cipher for a more general sense of corruption, the "seclusion and secrecy" he wrote about with regard to Wilde and which dominates *Dubliners*. Perhaps Joyce was playing the *enfant terrible*, looking to see just how much he could get away with at Russell's expense. There's certainly no doubt that the young Joyce was unsettled and intrigued by what we have come to call sexuality, and there has been much critical censure of the graphic and often obscene detail he put in his letters to Nora. Regarding this, however, there is a point at which we can know too much about a writer's life – a case-in-point being the opprobrium heaped on Philip Larkin after the publication of his letters, and which seems now to have made people shy of admitting the fact that Larkin is a great and humane writer. Furthermore, if in everything he wrote Joyce aimed to challenge and undermine the assumptions of Victorian Britain, and to expose the hypocrisy at the heart of its social mores, then stories like 'The Sisters' and 'An Encounter' at least bring into the open what everyone knew about but which, like Old Cotter, were too afraid to openly discuss. That Joyce met with this hypocrisy first-hand is apparent from the struggle to have 'An Encounter' published. In the crisis that surrounded publication of *Dubliners*, the subject matter of this story in particular was a problem. Padraic Colum pronounced it "a terrible story", and Joyce's friend Thomas Kettle – an intellectual Catholic and a Member of Parliament killed while fighting in the British Army in 1916 – denounced it outright. When Joyce pointed out to him that it was he who had taken part in the events narrated in the story, Kettle agreed that "we have all met him" (meaning "the queer old josser" the two boys meet in an open field) but that the story remained "beyond anything in its outspokenness" he had ever read.

That the priest's last illness is meant to represent the wider paralysis of Irish society is clear, and makes it all the more surprising that the story was accepted with no changes other than the name of the priest's parish. Joyce was paid a sovereign and the story was published on 13th August, the first anniversary of his mother's death, under the pseudonym of 'Stephen Daedalus'.

The *Irish Homestead* was to publish two more of Joyce's stories: 'Eveline', which tells the story of a young woman who has to decide whether to abandon her ageing and increasingly abusive father and run away and marry a sailor, Frank, bound for Buenos Ayres [sic]; and 'After the Race', a fictionalised portrait of the annual Gordon-Bennett automobile race which was held in Ireland on 2nd July 1903. They were to be the only examples of his prose that Joyce was successful in getting published until 1914, and the last things he ever wrote in Ireland before leaving for Trieste with Nora in October 1904. It seems prophetic, therefore, that both stories should be about illusion and disenchantment, the lure of foreign countries, and the chafing terrors of Irish life with its hidebound insularity. In 'Eveline', we are told how the girl's mother ends her "life of commonplace sacrifice ... in final craziness":

> She trembled as she heard again her mother's voice saying constantly with foolish insistence:
> – Derevaun Seraun! Derevaun Seraun!
> She stood up in a sudden impulse of terror. Escape! She must escape! Frank would save her. He would give her life, perhaps love, too. But she wanted to live. Why should she be unhappy?
> [p. 33]

The aperture of Joyce's interest in the downtrodden of Ireland widens in 'After the Race', where "The cars came scudding in towards Dublin, running evenly like pellets in the groove of the Naas Road ... careering homeward ... through this channel of poverty and inaction [.] Now and again the clumps of people raised the cheer of the gratefully oppressed."

It was to be 10 exasperating years before *Dubliners* was published in full – years when Joyce's manuscript was rejected, accused of blasphemy and libel, and even burned. By the time it appeared in print Joyce was known and admired as the poet of *Chamber Music*, praised by reviewers for its "ease and simplicity", "music and quaintness", and for being "simple", "pretty", "alluring". As a novelist, meanwhile, he was just beginning to receive credit for being the author of *A Portrait*, the opening chapters of which had started to be serialised in the *Egoist* in February 1914, chapters which deal with the earliest memories and experiences of Stephen Dedalus. Nothing that Joyce had thus far published could have prepared readers for the unsparing and uncompromising vision of Dublin life contained in *Dubliners*. Of those voices that condemned the book, while acknowledging its author's talents, this from an unsigned review in the *Athenaeum* is typical:

> The fifteen short stories ... are nothing if not naturalistic. In some ways, indeed, they are unduly so: at least three would have been better buried in oblivion. Life has so much that is beautiful, interesting, educative, amusing, that we do not readily pardon those who insist upon its more sordid and baser aspects.

Of course there were others more attune to the significance and scale of Joyce's achievement: "the maturity, the individual poise and force of these stories are astonishing"; "The author understands the technique of his craft to perfection"; "this is a book to recommend, evidently written by a man of broad sympathies and much human understanding"; and "One must be a great artist to treat events so simply". Even in the midst of such praise, however, there was one persistent cavil: that Joyce should have turned his undoubted artistry to more 'suitable' material. Why, then, did Joyce write about *what* he did in the *way* that he did?

Joyce's own response to such questions was unequivocal: "My intention was to write a chapter of the moral history of my country and I chose Dublin for the scene because that city seemed to me the centre of paralysis." Clear and to the point as this is, it should alert us to the fact that Joyce's aim was both aesthetic and moral; that his writing style, what he himself described as having a "scrupulous meanness", is directed less to telling a story than interpreting the facts. In short, there is something forensic about *Dubliners*, as though "the odour of ashpits and old weeds and offal" that hangs over the stories was actually the whiff of formaldehyde. It is not for nothing that the book begins with a story that includes a wake for a priest and ends with snow "general all over Ireland ... falling faintly through the universe and faintly falling, like the descent of their last end, upon all the living and the dead."

However, our response to the book undergoes a subtle shift if we read it not so much as a collection of stories and character sketches but as a novel, a novel in which the central character is Dublin itself. Looked at in this light, and the book becomes less about Ireland than about a certain kind, or kinds, of Irishness: urban, Catholic, largely working or lower-middle-class, not particularly well educated, spiritually and economically depressed, artistically parochial, reliant on alcohol, and almost without exception lonely and frightened. The wider Ireland, as in *A Portrait* and *Ulysses*, appears as a bit part: it is present in 'The Dead', but only in terms of a hopelessly idealised, and ultimately futile, form of romantic love. That Dublin is used to exemplify Ireland leads us to conclude that each character typifies an aspect of Dublin. Just as the pub landlord Earwicker in *Finnegans Wake* (to borrow a phrase from Walt Whitman) contains multitudes, so Joyce's aim in *Dubliners* is to show how Ireland, and what is meant by being Irish, is far from homogenous. Even when their lives are apparently similar, each character in *Dubliners* turns towards us a different aspect of urban, if not metropolitan, life. As we will see with special regard to *Ulysses*, and as Edmund Wilson suggested in his 1931 essay on Joyce, the texture of Joyce's fiction is intrinsically bound up with Dublin. It is, as Wilson says, "animated by a complex inexhaustible life: we revisit it as we do a city, where we come more and more to recognise faces, to understand personalities, to grasp relations, currents and interests."

In a letter to Grant Richards in 1906, Joyce drew his intended publisher's attention to this aspect of the book:

> I have tried to present [Dublin] to the indifferent public under four of its aspects: childhood, adolescence, maturity and public life. The stories are arranged in this order.

From the beginning, then, Joyce intended the book to have an overall shape and coherence that belied the more usual randomness of a collection of short stories. And though the stories were not written in the order in which they were published, there is little doubt that Joyce was working to a plan. As the book stands, then, 'The Sisters',

'An Encounter' and 'Araby' are linked to childhood; 'Eveline', 'After the Race', 'Two Gallants' and 'The Boarding House' are to do with adolescence; 'A Little Cloud', 'Counterparts', 'Clay' and 'A Painful Case' are the stories of maturity; and 'Ivy Day in the Committee Room', 'A Mother' and 'Grace' are to do with public life. Of course things are rarely so simple with Joyce. To take 'The Boarding House', for example, the story can only be linked with adolescence if we assume that the central character is Polly rather than Mrs Mooney or Mr Doran. Joyce's schema, then, was flexible enough to allow for ambiguity.

That Joyce even considered choosing Dublin as the setting for his "moral history" was in itself a radical departure. For if English writers from Shakespeare to Dickens took it for granted that their writing could and should focus on the teeming metropolitan life of London, Irish writers had predominantly looked to rural Ireland for inspiration. By his own admission, Joyce knew little of such a life, describing himself as a "lazy Dubliner who does not travel much and knows his country only by hearsay." It was a stance which, though he admired their writings enormously, left him at odds with, and distrustful of, the leading members of the Irish literary revival – Yeats, Russell, Lady Gregory and Synge – and drew him closer to a European writer such as the Norwegian dramatist Ibsen who wrote about modern life in urban settings and who weren't afraid to deal openly with the economic, sexual and political realities of the world. In the words of Seamus Deane, Joyce's project was "the production of a writing that is not embedded in or reducible to the categories of earlier Irish experience." In all of Joyce, the focus is on the present, the here-and-now. "The past," Stephen Dedalus states, "is consumed in the present and the present is living only because it brings forth the future."

Ironically, *Dubliners* is rank with the past. It is his unfulfilled past that leaves Mr James Duffy "perfectly silent" and alone at the end of 'A Painful Case', and it is the memory of Ireland's unsatisfied desire for independence that weighs heavily on the canvassers in 'Ivy Day In The Committee Room' as they mourn the anniversary of the death of Parnell while fantasising about him rising Christ-like from the tomb, or like Tom Finnegan roused by the smell of whiskey at his own wake. In 'A Little Cloud' the central character is caught between his "present joy" at meeting with an old friend who has made good on the London Press and the vague feeling that he, too, could have been a writer – though a poet and not "a tawdry journalist". 'The Dead' ends with a husband and wife's marriage strained to breaking point by her involuntary memories of a young man from her youth; and in 'Eveline' a young woman seems doomed to a life that mirrors that of her own dead mother. In addition to these isolated examples, Dublin is itself condemned, ancient-mariner-like, to tell its history over and over. A shadow of its former self, the city is now only "the gaunt spectral mansions in which the old nobility of Dublin had roistered". Even the opulence and seasonal bonhomie of the Morkan sisters in 'The Dead' takes place in rented accommodation above a corn factor's premises.

If Dublin's citizens and architecture are in thrall to the past – the grand vistas of historical consciousness or the more precarious slivers of personal reminiscence – then the names of the city and its institutions are no less imbued with the narrative of Empire and colonialism. That Joyce is at such pains to spell this out is surely a deliberate harking back to the ancient bardic tradition which R.F. Foster describes as having "studied, discussed and referenced [the terrain]: every place had its legend and its own identity. *Dindsenchas*, the celebration of place-names, was a feature of this poetic topography; what endured was the mythic landscape, providing escape and inspiration."

What endured in turn-of-the-twentieth-century Dublin, however, was an identity that replaces poetry with the cold comfort of the city's colonial status: characters live in and pass through Great Britain Street, North Richmond Street, Buckingham Street, Kingstown Station, Rutland Square, Duke's Lawn, George's Street, Ely Place and many other imported names. The centrality of this act of naming to the wider significance of *Dubliners* cannot be underestimated, though it often relies on the reader's knowledge of Anglo-Irish history. In 'Two Gallants', for example, and as both Jeri Johnson and Terence Brown point out in their Introductions and Notes to, respectively, the Oxford and Penguin editions of *Dubliners*, the references to Dublin's architecture and street names lend the story a series of complex double meanings that implicate Irish history since the Ascendancy. Thus Rutland Square is named for the 18th-century Lord-Lieutenant of Ireland, and houses the 20th-century headquarters of the Orange Lodge. Kildare Street contains The Kildare Street Club, founded in 1782 to provide a "haven of Unionism in Ireland", a fact that only underlines the trenchant irony of the harpist, a symbol of Ireland, "playing to a little ring of listeners … the melody of *Silent, O Moyle*" – a song which, as Brown says, "alludes to the enchantment of the children of Lir in the Irish legend [condemning them] to wander, for many hundreds of years, over certain lakes and rivers in Ireland".

That the inclusion of real place names in Dubliners was an actual hindrance to its publication, with publishers arguing that they did not belong in a work of fiction, only adds to the sense of denial and fear operating in Ireland, and at which Joyce took pot-shots in his satirical broadside 'Gas from a Burner' (1912):

> Shite and onions! Do you think I'll print
> The name of the Wellington Monument,
> Sydney Parade and the Sandymount tram,
> Downes's cakeshop and Williams's jam?
> I'm damned if I do – I'm damned to blazes!
> No, ladies, my press shall have no share in
> So gross a libel in Stepmother Erin.

Joyce, then, continued to argue for the publication of the book as he had written it, and not in the form others might wish him to have. And the claims he made for the book were far reaching: "I seriously believe that you will retard the course of civilisation in Ireland by preventing the Irish people from having one good look at themselves in my nicely polished looking-glass". Elsewhere, Joyce asserted that the purpose of his writing was to compose a history of Ireland that would prove to be "the first step towards the spiritual liberation of my country". The only means of achieving this was an unsparing honesty: life in Dublin was for many "exceptionally violent; painful and violent" and "suffering from hemiplegia of the will". To use a different medical analogy, *Dubliners* was to apply a massive electrical shock to a patient who has gone into cardiac arrest.

The hindrances to such liberation are writ everywhere in Joyce's Dublin, though not always as clearly as in street or railway station names. And it is the revelation of these influences as they appear in Joyce's writing that brings us within the orbit of a crucial term: Epiphany.

Taken from the Greek *epiphaneia*, meaning 'appearance', the

Christian feast day of Epiphany is known to have been observed earlier than AD 194, and is therefore more ancient a ritual celebration than Christmas. While it principally refers to the coming of the Three Wise Men and the revelation of Christ to the Gentiles, the term is also used to commemorate the marriage at Cana at which Christ performed his first miracle. And though Joyce's use of the term did not strictly refer to a manifestation of godhead, there is no doubt that such a metaphorical meaning would have appealed to him.

Joyce's epiphanies can be understood as a revelation of the duplicitous workings of ideology. For alongside descriptions of the epiphany as a sudden "revelation of the whatness of a thing" and "the soul of the commonest object", Joyce also called them "little errors – mere straws in the wind – by which people betrayed the very things they were most careful to conceal". Though I will have more to say about the epiphany in relation to *A Portrait*, it is important to note that in many ways it is the epiphany that joins together all of Joyce's writings, from his notebook jottings in 1901-2 through to *Dubliners* and *Ulysses*. Above all it is the epiphany which gives rise to the unsparing realism of Joyce's writing, that aspect of his work that can be overlooked in favour of the verbal and imaginative flights of fancy that increasingly take over. It is the epiphany which grounds Joyce and his characters in the world as we ourselves know it. And it was the epiphany that gave rise to Joyce's often obsessive commitment to getting things right; a process which, as Jeri Johnson has commented, results in fact and fiction being so "intimately commingled ... that we find ourselves drawn to some discomforting questions" about who is more real: Joyce's fictional characters or the real, historical Dublin which they inhabit. It is a commitment to the "whatness of a thing" that can be seen as a justification for those aspects of Joyce's writing that his contemporaries found most difficult to stomach: the "horse piss and rotted straw" that calms Stephen's agitated heart in *A Portrait*; the frank description of the paralytic priest in 'The Sisters'; the unscrupulous Corley and Lenehan in 'Two Gallants'; the petty squabbles and connivance of the artistes in 'A Mother'; and the bringing home to Gabriel Conroy of the fact that his wife has lived a life about which he knows nothing.

While *A Portrait* is geared solely towards the epiphany as it pertains to the life of a budding writer, in *Dubliners* its function is more general and we find it used to link characters of a more prosaic nature. Always, however, it appears in relation to the making visible or audible the unseen or unspoken. For *Dubliners* is a book riddled with what can't or won't be said. That this is so is a hangover from that aspect of 19th-century Ireland written about by Willa Murphy, who sees the fact of colonialism as resulting in "a whole culture of concealment in Ireland." Murphy continues:

> When the majority of a population is excluded from public means of expression and protest, those political energies move underground, creating a smouldering subterranean culture beneath a surface of submission and silence.[1]

Thus Old Cotter's warnings about the priest in 'The Sisters' ebb into silence, as do the cries of the beaten and sobbing child at the end of 'Counterparts'. The "thick slice of plumcake" that Maria buys to take home to Joe's house in 'Clay' is spirited away unseen by a passenger on a tram; and we are left to infer exactly what the "queer old josser" in 'An Encounter' is up to. What links these disparate examples, however petty or sordid, is the fact that Dublin is an occupied city. Like the weeds that spring up between the paving stones in the Brussels of Conrad's *Heart of Darkness*, the presence of the British as an occupying force is everywhere, whether manifest in the "soldiers with brown baggages" that crowd the station at the North Wall in 'Eveline', or the threatening presence in 'The Boarding House' of Jack Mooney, "a hard case ... fond of using soldiers' obscenities". Empire and colonialism are also present in the most unlikely places: the comics which the boys read in 'An Encounter' – *The Union Jack*, *Pluck* and *The Halfpenny Marvel* – were all published in England and, as Terence Brown has noted, are there to suggest "the imperial vision of adventurous British boyhood that played a significant part in late-Victorian British culture". The "yellowing photograph" of the priest which hangs "on the wall above the broken harmonium" in 'Eveline' represents simply one among many Irish men and women who, voluntarily or otherwise, left Ireland in the 19th century for penal life in Australia. *Dubliners* is packed with authority figures of one kind or another, all trying to assert themselves over their fellow citizens: from fathers who beat their children, to mothers trying to palm their daughters off in marriage, or the "queer old josser" who recounts to the narrator of 'An Encounter' his fantasies of "chastising boys". Like him, and like the horse in Gabriel Conroy's humorous story in 'The Dead' which keeps walking round the statue of 'King Billy' in College Green, Joyce's characters are all "magnetised by some words of [their] own speech … slowly circling round and round in the same orbit".

One needn't go looking too hard for the root cause of much that is out of kilter in the lives of Joyce's Dubliners. From beginning to end – from the nudge-nudge, wink-wink of Old Cotter to Gabriel's vision of an Ireland impotent under its blanket of snow – the stories reveal a narrative of sexual antagonism and frustration. That there is an alternative to this isn't perhaps fully recognisable to us as readers until we encounter the "profane joy" of Stephen's provocatively sensuous epiphany on the beach in *A Portrait*. The hints are all there, however; hints that bring us close to Foucault's description of 19th-century sexuality as "restrained, mute and hypocritical".[2] Foucault, whose work on sexuality can be read as an instructive guide to much of the subtext of Joyce's fiction, goes on to define Victorian sexuality in phrases that make explicit much of what remains implicit in *Dubliners*: "the principle of secrecy [and] verbal decency sanitized one's speech".

Opposing itself to these forces of repression and inhibition is another kind of sexuality, one that refuses to limit and confine sexual practice to the home, to the parental bed. It is a sexuality which in *Dubliners* is feral and dangerous: the green-eyed man masturbating within sight of two young boys; Corley and the girl who go out by tram to a field in Donnybrook; and most dramatically of all, Gretta and Michael Furey outside together in the rain in Galway. It is a sexuality which, persecuted and driven underground, becomes distorted and profoundly destructive. Thus in *A Portrait* Stephen, terrorised by the promptings of his unconscious and the restrictions of his Catholic upbringing, writes long letters in which he confesses in detail "the sootcoated packet of pictures which he had hidden in the flue of the fireplace and in the presence of whose shameless or bashful wantonness he lay for hours sinning in thought and deed" and which, in a scene of genuine horror and self-loathing, come back to haunt him as a vision of his own personal hell which, in turn, reminds us of the dying priest in 'The Sisters' and the man in 'An Encounter':

> Goatish creatures with human faces, horneybrowed, lightly bearded and grey as indiarubber. … Soft language issued from their spittleless lips as they swished in slow circles round and round the field, winding hither and thither through the weeds … They moved in slow circles, circling closer and closer to enclose, to enclose, soft language issuing from their lips.
> [*A Portrait*, pp. 148-49]

What distorts Stephen's sexual energies is the clash between his instincts and the Catholic education that leaves him unable to see women as anything other than either 'Madonna' or 'Whore'. The female therefore presides over his imagination as either the Mother he must escape if he is to become a man, or the devouring Other who would (symbolically) castrate him. Though rarely so starkly expressed, the theme of masculine and feminine sexuality in *Dubliners* is also the focus of any number of anxieties. Against these forces of legislature, Joyce posits a position of ambiguity, one where the self cannot so narrowly be determined, and where the geographies of the unconscious are more free-floating. Thus in 'An Encounter' the man the boys meet in the field begins fantasising first about girls with their "nice soft hair" and later about giving boys "a good sound whipping"; in 'Eveline', one of only two good memories Eveline has of her father is his "putting on her mother's bonnet to make the children laugh"; in 'After the Race' "Villona played a waltz for Farley and Rivière, Farley acting as cavalier and Rivière as lady"; and in 'The Boarding House' Polly is able to say under cover of singing a music hall song what everyone already suspects: "I'm a … naughty girl./You needn't sham:/You know I am".

While such examples are a long way from Foucault's "polymorphous sexuality" (we shall have to wait until the Circe episode of *Ulysses* for that), nevertheless Joyce, like Foucault, is interested in the question:

> By what spiral did we come to affirm that sex is negated? What led us to show, ostentatiously, that sex is something we hide, to say it is something we silence?

That his characters' sexual lives are as narrow and bent on frustration as they are, simply provides another point-of-contact between Joyce's fiction and Foucault's philosophy, inasmuch as they show how "the least glimmer of truth is political". Foucault's words enjoy their correlative in something Joyce wrote in 1904 in an essay entitled 'A Portrait of the Artist': "these things be good which yet are corrupted". It is a phrase that re-focuses our attention on the morality of *Dubliners*, as well as reminding us of the use to which Joyce was intent on putting the epiphany.

Before leaving *Dubliners* for *A Portrait of the Artist as a Young Man*, I want to draw the reader's attention to the fact that the act of self-portraiture that commands centre-stage in the novel has, though in a simplified form, an important part to play in the stories. In 'The Sisters', for example, we can recognise in the adolescent boy and the unnamed narrator, and in the dead and dying priest a double-portrait of Joyce: for while the priest, as does Mr Duffy in 'A Painful Case', shares Joyce's Christian name, so the boy shares Joyce's fascination with language:

> Every night as I gazed up at the window I said softly to myself the word *paralysis*. It had always sounded strangely in my ears, like the word *gnomon* in the Euclid and the word *simony* in the Catechism. [p. 1]

Mention of Mr Duffy further reminds us that he, like Joyce, was keen to complete a translation of Gerhardt Hauptmann's play *Michael Kramer*, the difference being that while Mr Duffy abandons his version, Joyce went on to complete his. Such parallels have suggested themselves to other critics, with Hugh Kenner for one seeing connections between *Dubliners* and the mythical and religious archetypes of *A Portrait*: Jimmy Doyle in 'After the Race' is therefore "a possible Jimmy Joyce who remained in Dublin [and the] priest [in 'The Sisters'] is a frustrated St Stephen; Eveline a frustrated Dedalus." Once we start looking for such correspondences between Joyce's life in Dublin and that of his characters, we discover that they begin cropping up in almost every story – though never in an altogether straightforward way.

Arguably the closest Joyce comes to writing himself into *Dubliners* is in the book's final story, 'The Dead' where, in addition to those details Joyce borrows from his relationship with Nora and the jealousy he experienced when she told him about her love affairs in Galway, Gabriel is given certain other characteristics in which we can recognise Joyce: like Joyce, Gabriel wears his hair parted in the middle and needs glasses; he writes for the Dublin-based *Daily Telegraph*; looks to Europe and not the West of Ireland for his political and cultural influences; and, most tellingly, in the letter he remembers having written to Gretta during their courtship – "Why is it that words like these seem to me so dull and cold? Is it because there is no word tender enough to be your name?" – he quotes almost word for word a letter which Joyce had sent Nora in 1904. The great difference between Joyce and Gabriel, of course, is that by the time Joyce came to write 'The Dead' in 1906/7 he was no longer living in Dublin but in Rome. These projections of himself in fiction – the neurotic Duffy, the frustrated Chandler, the parasitic Lenehan and disenchanted Gabriel Conroy – are all partial versions of Joyce, a Joyce gone to seed, the writer who stayed languishing in Dublin. It is a harsh judgement, on himself and on Dublin.

Of course there is a great deal more to 'The Dead' than self-portraiture. Many critics would regard it as the single finest short story written in English, and there is no doubt that it marks a significant development in Joyce's prose fiction. Not only is it the longest story by some way in *Dubliners* but it is also the story in which we see Joyce successfully working on a larger scale. The characters are drawn with greater sympathy than elsewhere in the book, and the view of Dublin it presents is less harsh and insistently cynical. Unlike a number of the other stories we aren't left to condemn the actions or choices of a single character. Whatever flaws Gabriel has they are not on the same scale as those of the emotionally impotent Mr Duffy, the wretched Corley and Lenehan, or the 'pimping' Mrs Mooney. In many ways these characters are recognisable 'villains' – though their crimes are petty and the only comeuppance they receive is to continue living the lives they have made for themselves. Gabriel, on the other hand, is sensitive and cultured. It is true that he's a little too preoccupied with himself and is a bit of a stuffed-shirt, but he has some sense of the limitations of the life he is leading and has the energy to do something about it. He rejects Irish Nationalism and the movement to reintroduce Gaelic as the first language, and prefers holidaying in Europe to the West of Ireland. It is a philosophy that gets him into hot water with the nationalistic Miss Ivors:

— And why do you go to France and Belgium, said Miss Ivors, instead of visiting your own land?
— Well, said Gabriel, it's partly to keep in touch with the language and partly for a change.
— And haven't you your own language to keep in touch with — Irish? asked Miss Ivors.
— Well, said Gabriel, if it comes to that, you know, Irish is not my language. [p. 189]

Miss Ivors continues to goad Gabriel, until he snaps at her: " – O, to tell you the truth, retorted Gabriel suddenly, I'm sick of my own country, sick of it."

The irony of this, particularly in light of what we know of Joyce's close affinity with what Gabriel has to say and his reasons for saying it, is that ultimately 'The Dead' suggests that Gabriel is personally lacking in aspects of what the West of Ireland popularly represented: passion, spontaneity, mystery. In short, Gabriel is not in touch with those aspects of Irish cultural and psychological life which, in Matthew Arnold's terms, are essentially feminine and prone to "extravagance and exaggeration". We are therefore left to conclude that what Gabriel lacks is the passion and fire which, for Gretta, is idealised by her dead lover in Galway. Her attachment to Michael Furey may in one sense be as sentimental as the words of the song *The Lass of Aughrim* which she remembers him singing to her and which Bartell D'Arcy recites at the party; nevertheless it is an emotion powerful enough to distance her from her husband, and to alienate and isolate Gabriel from what he thought were the assurances of his own life. It is a sentiment strong enough to make her turn away from the present and to think about what might have been. For Gabriel the knowledge that his wife harbours these memories and feelings for a mere boy who worked at the local gasworks crushes the life within him:

A vague terror seized Gabriel at this answer as if, at that hour when he had hoped to triumph, some impalpable and vindictive being was coming against him, gathering forces against him in its vague world. [pp. 221-22]

For all that *Dubliners* excludes rural Ireland from its pages, it returns in the final pages of the book and wrecks the life of the one character we had hoped might escape the labyrinth of Irish customs and complaints.

In conclusion two other 'self-portraits' seem to me worthy of comment, each offering an insight not only into Joyce's state of mind when writing these stories but into the complex relationship between life and art that was to remain the cantus firmus of all his mature fiction.

In 'Eveline', written in the immediate weeks preceding his elopement with Nora, we might see the central character, torn between her loyalties for her family and her need to escape, as a version of Joyce himself. Read in such a light, we can see Eveline as a necessary sacrifice: she must stay behind in order that Joyce can leave. What is certain is that the self-portraits that haunt and shadow the pages of *Dubliners* do so because of the fact that they arise from Joyce's profound fear of what might happen to him if he remained in Ireland. Thus in Little Chandler from 'A Little Cloud' we are faced with a man who retains some slight ambition to be a poet and who imagines the English critics praising his poetry: "Mr Chandler has the gift of easy and graceful verse ... A wistful sadness pervades these poems ... The Celtic note". Though Joyce satirises Chandler's day-dreams and the ambitions of all Irish writers who struck 'The Celtic note', the fact remains that when Joyce's own first book of poems was published in 1907, reviewers discussed the book in phrases not dissimilar to those imagined by Chandler: "Mr Joyce flows in a clear delicious stream"; "Light and evanescent, pretty and fragile [h]is muse is a gentle tender spirit that knows smiles and tears, the rain, the dew and the morning sun". The important thing to note, however, is that Chandler never sits down to write a poem. His remains a portrait of the *poete manqué*. For though *Dubliners* contains plenty of descriptions of artisans and artistes, the artist is absent from its pages. For that act of portraiture to take place Joyce had to leave Dublin and enter a voluntary self-exile.

Footnotes

[1] 'Maria Edgeworth and the Aesthetics of Secrecy', *Ideology and Ireland in the Nineteenth Century* (ed.) Tadhg Foley and Seán Ryder (Four Courts Press: Dublin, 1998), pp. 45-54.

[2] Michel Foucault, *The Will to Knowledge: The History of Sexuality*, Vol. I (Penguin: London, 1998).

3

Staring at the Sun:
A Portrait of the Artist as a Young Man

To discuss the genesis of *A Portrait of the Artist as a Young Man* means going back to before Joyce had begun work on any of the stories in *Dubliners*. It also means recounting some details of Joyce's family life and circumstances, and his movements.

On 1st December 1902, having graduated from University College and subsequently abandoned Dublin's Royal University Medical School, Joyce left Ireland for Paris with the stated aim of resuming his medical studies abroad. His real motivation, as Richard Ellmann has commented, was very different:

> Migration to Paris was flamboyant; other Irish writers, Shaw, Wilde, and Yeats, had gone to London, and he would do something else. Paris would separate him further than London from familiar things, and he would advance upon Europe with the missionary zeal (though not the piety) of his fellow Celts, 'fiery Columbanus, the subtle doctor John Scotus, and Fiacre, eponymous saint of the cab drivers'.

Joyce's, then, was a secular pilgrimage to the city which had been at the heart of Europe's Middle Ages when, as he was later to write in 'Ireland: Island of Saints and Sages', Ireland itself had been "a true centre of intellectualism and sanctity, that spread its culture and stimulating energy through the continent." As Ellmann suggests, it was to the renaissance of such Celtic energies which Joyce intended to devote himself. The fact, however, was that Joyce was unprepared for life as a medical student in Paris – his French simply wasn't good enough. Further complications followed when, in April 1903, he received a telegram from his father: "Mother dying come home

Father".

May Joyce died in August 1903 at the relatively young age of 44, exhausted by 15 pregnancies between 1881 and 1893 and the subsequent demands of raising the 10 children who survived infancy and coping with the increasingly erratic behaviour of her husband and her eldest son. During her final hours she lay in a coma with her family gathered round her praying. Despite the exhortations of his uncle, John Murray (Uncle Charles in *A Portrait*) Joyce and his brother Stanislaus refused to kneel. Though he never repented the action, it continued to dog his conscience, as a similar refusal does Stephen Dedalus in *Ulysses*:

> – You could have knelt down, damn it, Kinch, when your dying mother asked you, Buck Mulligan said. [T]o think of your mother begging you with her last breath to kneel down and pray for her. And you refused. There is something sinister in you ... [p. 5]

(Incidentally, we might wonder how great a part Joyce's guilt played in the relationship between Anna Livia Plurabelle and her writer son, Shem the Penman, in *Finnegans Wake*, who she refers to as "you firstborn and firstfruit of woe, branded sheep, pick of the wastepaperbaskel".)

His mother's death hit Joyce hard. It also prompted a great burst of creative energy. From 3rd September to 19th November 1903 some 14 unsigned reviews by Joyce appeared in the *Daily Telegraph* (the same Dublin-based newspaper that Gabriel Conroy was to write for), and early in 1904 he wrote at one sitting an essay-cum-short story he called 'A Portrait of the Artist', and which was rejected by *Dana*, a new journal of 'independent thought'. "I handed it back to him," said W.K. Magee, the journal's editor and co-founder, "with the timid observation that I did not care to publish what was to myself incomprehensible ... I imagine that what he showed me was some early attempt in fiction." Indeed it was. And over the following ten years 'A Portrait of the Artist' was to evolve first into *Stephen Hero* (26 chapters of a planned 63 of which were written between 1904 and 1907) before being re-cast as *A Portrait of the Artist as a Young Man*.

It is worth recalling, then, that contemporary readers would have read the earliest chapters of *A Portrait* some five months before the first publication of *Dubliners*. The differences between the two books must have seemed extreme. For while *Dubliners* remained recognisably rooted in 19th-century realism, *A Portrait* was deemed to be, in the words of a reader's report commissioned in 1916 by Duckworth & Co, "too discursive, formless, unrestrained, and ugly things, ugly words, are too prominent". Such, too, was the conclusion of an unsigned review in *Everyman* in 1917 when the novel was first published in book form:

> [*A Portrait*] is an astonishingly powerful and extraordinarily dirty study of the upbringing of a young man by Jesuits, which ends – so far as we have been at all able to unravel the meaning of the impressionist ending – with his insanity ... Mr Joyce is a clever novelist, but we feel he would be really at his best in a treatise on drains.

Joyce's fictional writings enjoyed long gestations. This is perhaps truest of *A Portrait*. From as early as 1901 Joyce had been writing fragments of dialogue and what, for want of a better term, we might call 'prose poems' that were ultimately to find a place within the novel. The use to which he put a number of these becomes immediately clear when, looking at the first of the 40 epiphanies that have survived (it seems that at one point there were at least 71 such sketches), we come across a scene familiar as one of Stephen Dedalus' earliest memories:

[Bray: in the parlour of the house
in Martello Terrace]

Mr Vance – (*comes in with a stick*) ... O, you know,
     he'll have to apologise, Mrs Joyce.
Mrs Joyce – O yes ... Do you hear that, Jim?
Mr Vance – Or else – if he doesn't – the eagles'll
     come and pull out his eyes.
Mrs Joyce – O, but I'm sure he will apologise.
Joyce – (*under the table, to himself*)
     – Pull out his eyes,

Apologise,
Apologise,
Pull out his eyes.

Apologise,
Pull out his eyes,
Pull out his eyes,
Apologise.

With only the slightest of changes we are plunged into the opening pages of *A Portrait*, with its account of a sensitive boy's confrontation with authority and guilt. Like the *trouvailles* ('found objects') that the Surrealists used for some of their artworks, these fragments of dialogue and evocations of mood and emotion came to serve Joyce right up until the completion of *Ulysses* (in which four of the epiphanies appear) and even *Finnegans Wake* (in which there is one). I will have more to say about Joyce's interesting use of fragments a little later. For now, though, it is important to note that the epiphanies, by turns dramatic and poetic, underpin all that Joyce was to achieve as a novelist.

Joyce clearly came to see the epiphany as a moment of artistic vision gleaned from the everyday; what, in a different context, Walter Benjamin, called "profane illuminations" and which Hugh Kenner points to as having being essential to Joyce's "sense of fact". By the time, then, that he came to be writing *Stephen Hero* Joyce was ready to integrate the epiphany into his protagonist's developing sense of himself as an artist:

> By an epiphany he [Stephen] meant a sudden spiritual manifestation, whether in the vulgarity of speech or a gesture or in a memorable phrase of the mind itself. He believed that it was for the man of letters to record these epiphanies with extreme care, seeing that they themselves are the most delicate and evanescent of moments.

The danger with such moments, as Joyce came to recognise, is that their very intensity gives birth to a subjectivity that can be overwhelming – a little like standing too close to a painting so that all you can see is a blur of colour lacking form. The experience may in itself be a powerful one; what is missing (and no pun is intended) is the ability to see the whole picture. There is also the problem of how to structure these random and isolated items into an artistic whole. What Joyce needed, then, was the sense of objectivity and perspective – not to say humility – which, in *Ulysses*, Stephen ridicules his younger self for having lacked:

> Remember your epiphanies written on green oval leaves, deeply deep, copies to be sent if you died to all the great libraries of the world, including Alexandria? Someone was to read them there after a few thousand years[.] [p. 34]

What helped Joyce achieve this, and what the reviewer from the *Everyman* didn't recognise, was the increasingly important element of irony in Joyce's writing that gives each event in *A Portrait* a two-fold meaning: Stephen's experiences in the present moment, and the significance of the event in the wider context of the novel. The latter, as Stephen is not reading the novel of his own life, is left to the reader to piece together. On first encounter this isn't always easy, given the intensity of Stephen's imagination and the quivering sensitivity of his feelings. It can be difficult for the reader not to take Stephen's word for things.

I remember first being handed *A Portrait* in the sixth-form at school and being in awe of Stephen. In fact, as I, like Stephen, attended an all-boys Catholic Grammar School and was beginning to write what I (wrongly) thought were poems, I empathised with him to such a degree that I'm still unable to distinguish some of the things I recall about being aged sixteen or seventeen from certain scenes in the novel. I mention this only because it seems to me now that the empathy I felt with Stephen must in some small way have mirrored Joyce's. And just as my subsequent readings of the novel – and I am now more than twice my age when I first picked up the book – have inevitably brought a greater degree of objectivity to what I think about Stephen and the novel, so too Joyce needed to distance himself from the emotional and intellectual upheavals he himself experienced when Stephen's age. I still admire Stephen, but now what I feel towards him is closer to being the emotions of a concerned uncle rather than a younger sibling. Not that this growing sense of detachment is all down to my advancing years; no, simply that the profound ambivalences of Joyce's portrait of Stephen for a long while

33

passed me by. In other words, I was reading only that aspect of the novel that reflected my own experiences, experiences that Hugh Kenner bluntly, though appropriately, defines as "a highly original pastiche of the decadent sensibility, with a tang of smoking lamps and relished corruption." Similarly, then, with Joyce's epiphanies which, when read in isolation, are simply passages of adolescent purple prose. In the context of the complex narratative strategies of *A Portrait*, however, they become transformed into manifestations of Stephen's inner self rather being accepted as accurate renderings of actual events. It was the discovery of this – his own, so to speak, Theory of Relativity – that enabled Joyce to initiate that complex to-ing and fro-ing between the external world and the human (un)conscious that was to become an increasing pre-occupation of his work.

A Portrait is about precisely this relationship between subjectivity and objectivity, a fact that contributes much to the difficulty of reading and re-reading the novel. Central to many readers' experience of the book will be the effort to understand what exactly Joyce intends us to think of Stephen Dedalus. For on this, it will seem to most readers, our final judgement of the work depends. And there is no escaping him. Everything that happens in the novel is registered in terms of Stephen, and all the novel's events are important solely in terms of how they contribute to his developing artistic sensibility. This can also be said of Richard Rowan, the central character of Joyce's only surviving play, *Exiles* (he wrote another, *My Brilliant Career,* now lost, when he was 18*)*, an Irish writer who returns to Dublin after a nine year exile in Italy with his common-law wife, Bertha, only to have his relations with her challenged by the re-appearance of one of her ex-lovers. Clearly Joyce was basing the play partly on his life in exile with Nora and the bouts of jealousy – more often than not unprovoked and groundless – that he suffered when separated from her, and his own anxieties about returning to Ireland. It is the very closeness of the fictional material to the marrow of Joyce's life despite the flashes of brilliance that illumine the play and make it a remark-ably intense piece of writing, that ultimately leads us to judge *Exiles* an artistic failure. Unlike Stephen, and the many-layered use to which Joyce puts his epiphanies in *A Portrait*, Richard Rowan remains too close to Joyce. That the play is a failure, though, offers a fascinating insight into why Joyce took so long to write *A Portrait*: what he needed was the clarity of vision which, at that stage of his life, could only be gained from letting his adolescent passions cool and getting the hell out of Dublin.

At the start of the novel the young child's psychological dependency on his parents for a sense of identity is brought acutely to life by the free-floating grammar and syntax of Joyce's prose, and the imagistic fragments of the child's developing consciousness:

> His father told him that story: his father looked at him through a glass: he had a hairy face.
> He was baby tuckoo. The moocow came down the road where Betty Byrne lived: she sold lemon platt.
>
> *O, the wild rose blossoms*
> *On the little green place.*
>
> He sang that song. That was his song. [p. 3]

Who exactly is being referred to by the repeated use of "he" and "his"; and who has the hairy face, Stephen or his father? What is the glass through which Stephen is looked at: a monocle? a window? the bottom of a whisky glass? Are the moocow and Betty Byrne real people or characters from a story the child is being told? And above all, who is speaking: the child, an adult remembering his childhood, the father, a narrator, or some mixture of them all? What is clear is that Stephen's sense of himself is acutely subjective. If we read this passage for biographical facts, we will be disappointed. We aren't told how old the boy is, when and where he was born, or anything about his family background. As far as the reader is concerned, Stephen is 'born' at the moment he becomes conscious of language as it relates to himself. The novel declares from the off that the portrait we are being shown does not have an existence anterior or exterior to language and the pages of the book. A similar point is made at the end of the penultimate episode of *Ulysses* when Bloom drops off to sleep, a sleep that is represented as "•", or a single drop of ink. What Joyce is foregrounding, then, is the fact that identity is fluid and dependent on language. In other words, only when Stephen can say 'I' (and know what it means) will he have become himself. What follows is his journey, uncompleted at the novel's end, to not only say but write 'I', and to do so free of the various influences and restrictions that, in Stephen's own words, hold the soul back from flight. Stephen must learn that the self is plural. This is brought home to readers in Stephen's own description of his father, a description that is intended to be critical but which contains a truth of which Stephen is as yet unaware:

> Stephen began to enumerate glibly his father's attributes.
> – A medical man, an oarsman, a tenor, an amateur actor, a shouting politician, a small landlord, a small investor, a drinker, a good fellow, a storyteller, somebody's secretary, something in a distillery, a taxgatherer, a bankrupt and at present a praiser of his own past. [p. 262]

The multiple characters of *Dubliners* have here been replaced by a single figure in a way that comes close to Joyce's response to Frank Budgen's question as to who was the "complete man in literature":

> Ulysses is son to Laertes, but he is father to Telemachus, husband to Penelope, lover of Calypso, companion in arms of the Greek warriors around Troy and King of Ithaca. [H]e was a war dodger who tried to evade military service [but] once at war the conscientious objector became a jusqu'auboutist. When the others wanted to abandon the siege he insisted on staying till Troy should fall. [H]e was the first gentleman in Europe [and] an inventor too.

As a work of fiction, *A Portrait* tantalisingly straddles the genres of the *Bildungsroman* – a novel about the growth and development of an individual – and the *Kunstlerroman* – a novel depicting the growth and development of an artist. Title aside, it is difficult to know how seriously we are to take Stephen's claims to being an artist. For though we witness the first splutterings of what might be evidence of an artistic 'calling', neither in *A Portrait* or *Ulysses* do we see him accomplishing anything of significance. This is deliberate. What Joyce is paralleling in Stephen's awakening consciousness is the possibility of an Irish renaissance. To invest Stephen with too great a gift would be to sever the important links between him and the Irish 'race' which, at the novel's end, despite the proceeding struggle, he finally acknowledges kinship. Hence we observe

Stephen's attempts at writing poetry, his formulation of a coherent aesthetics and, in the novel's closing pages, a diary. In other words, Stephen moves from a point where others (i.e. the third-person of the novel's opening pages) narrate his life to becoming the author of his own destiny (i.e. the first-person of his diary). That this contradicts Stephen's own theories about art – that, like *Dubliners*, it should move from first- to third- person – shouldn't detract from the seriousness of his enterprise. Stephen isn't in any simplistic sense a photographic likeness of Joyce; but in the ferocity of his Ibsenesque rejection of everything we use to orientate ourselves in the world there is a great deal of Joyce's youthful anger:

> I will not serve that in which I no longer believe whether it call itself my home, my fatherland or my church: and I will try to express myself in some mode of life or art as freely as I can and as wholly as I can, using for my defence the only arms I allow myself to use – silence, exile, and cunning. [pp. 268-69]

The important thing to note here is the phrase "whether it call itself", in which Stephen questions the veracity and authority of the very concepts he is rejecting. We should also note that Stephen is here assuming silence, associated entirely with the negative in *Dubliners*, as a weapon, a deliberate tactic and means of resisting those things I earlier banded together under the term ideology. His doing so, however, is hardly unique in an occupied country where, over the course of the previous century, a whole culture of conspiracy and silence was spawned and which saw the emergence of such movements as the Defenders, United Irishmen, Whiteboys, Rightboys, Ribbonmen, and Molly Maguires. Founded on a combination of secrecy and terror, these revolutionary societies worked towards political change in Ireland. As Willa Murphy has commented, "Nocturnal meetings, ritual oaths, millenarian slogans, coded haircuts and clothing, secret handshakes, passwords, code-names and cross-dressing, combined with threats of violence against the ruling class, created an Irish landscape of mystery and terrifying inscrutability". Neither were such movements confined to the 19th century. Between 1912-1922 (between, that is, the House of Lords blocking Lloyd George's Home Rule Bill and the end of the Irish

Civil War) numerous private 'volunteer' armies were formed in the north and south of Ireland in open defiance of the British government.

Stephen adopts silence as a tactic of resistance, and a refusal to divulge his beliefs. His is a situation where honesty is not the best policy – hence his retreat from discussing politics, art and religion with his peers into the writing of a 'secret' diary. Silence, then, offers a form of liberation from the identity and boundaries set on him by others. Stephen, then, must learn to quote himself. So too must Ireland. For as Seamus Deane has said in his Introduction to the novel, "Ireland must find its own language or be doomed to quote itself as a stereotype in a language that belonged to others." In this Stephen is remarkably successful. Indeed it is difficult to think of another single character from a 20th-century novel whose words are so powerfully aphoristic and carry such authority. When we think of Stephen, it is less a physical likeness that comes to mind as a series of self-defining portraits in words:

> This race and this country and this life produced me ... I shall express myself as I am. [p. 220]

> When the soul of a man is born in this country there are nets flung at it to hold it back from flight. You talk to me of nationality, language, religion. I shall try to fly by those nets. [p. 220]

> I desire to press in my arms the loveliness which has not yet come into the world. [p. 273]

> Welcome, O life! I go to encounter for the millionth time the reality of experience and to forge in the smithy of my soul the uncreated conscience of my race. [pp. 275-76]

> Old father, old artificer, stand me now and ever in good stead. [p. 276]

These final words, the closing sentence of the novel, bring us to the central paradox of *A Portrait*: that while it presents us with a young man trying to assert his own unique individuality, as a literary character he is determined by his name. In the same way that a character in, say, a medieval morality play is simply a personification of such abstractions as flesh, gluttony, lechery, sloth, pride, envy, hope, charity, riches, and strength, or a character in certain of Brecht's parables – Mother Courage, for example – are essentially defined by their names, so Stephen Dedalus is fated to assume certain aspects of both the first Christian martyr and the mythical architect of the labyrinth and the inventor of human-powered flight after which he is called. He is also fated to be neither, but to be a young Irish Catholic struggling to become an artist against the head winds of colonialism, religion and Nationalism.

The strangeness of Stephen's name is commented on, quizzed and ridiculed by a succession of characters, both in *A Portrait* and in *Ulysses*. It is a name, with its overpowering symbolic connotations, by which Stephen himself appears burdened: he refuses to accept the role of Irish martyr, and seems unsure right to the end of the novel whether he is Daedalus or his son, Icarus, who drowned after the wings his father fashioned for him from wax and feathers melted after he flew too close to the sun – a sun, by the way, which was popularly figured as never setting on the British Empire.

In figuring such issues in his central character's name, Joyce has created a labyrinth of cultural references from which Stephen must struggle to escape. For while he is both Icarus and Daedalus he is also Lucifer, the "bright one" or Isaiah's "son of the morning", who was cast out of heaven for rejecting God's authority and refusing to serve Him. The irony of this becomes all the greater given Stephen's overbearing sense of his own Messianic status as the novel draws to a close. This is spelled out in his diary entry for "21 March, morning" where he writes of Cranly as John the Baptist to his own Christ. We might say that it is not Ireland so much as his author who casts the nets of "nationality, language, religion" over Stephen.

Part of what Joyce is doing, then, is asking questions about the very notion of a literary character, carrying out an act of Derridean deconstruction whereby identity is recognised as being socially-constructed, and where 'character' has no independent status and functions merely as a by-product of historical and cultural forces. Thus the more Stephen struggles to free himself from Ireland and its influences, the more enmeshed he becomes. Only at the novel's close, when he refers to his 'race' does he wake up to the fact that he is inescapably a part of history. In such moments of epiphany lie stored the promise of whatever freedom from intimidation Stephen can hope to muster.

It may be helpful at this point to return to another aspect of Barthes' argument in *Writing Degree Zero*, one which will allow us to see the fuller symbolic and metaphorical connotations of Stephen's name.

Responding to the question "What is Writing?", Barthes says that it is the point at which language and style meet. More particularly, he uses a metaphor that might seem to us particularly apt when thinking about a character who is acutely conscious that the language he speaks has been historically imposed on him and his homeland. Barthes writes:

> A language is therefore a horizon, and style a vertical dimension, which together map out for the writer a Nature, since he does not choose either. The language functions negatively, as the initial limit of the possible; style is a Necessity which binds the writer's humour to his form of expression. In the former, he finds a familiar History, in the latter, a familiar personal past.

If Barthes had been writing with *A Portrait* and Stephen Dedalus in mind, he could not so succinctly have summed up the central argument of the novel: that Stephen, and by inference Ireland, will only become free of English authority by discovering within the English language that "familiar personal past" which goes against the grain of history; finding it, in terms used by Stephen Hero when describing the epiphany, in "a sudden spiritual manifestation ... in the vulgarity of speech".

There are close parallels between such perceived 'vulgarity' and the use to which Joyce puts his own autobiography in *A Portrait*. For example: like Stephen, Joyce attended Clongowes Wood, Belvedere, and University College Dublin; they share addresses in Bray, Blackrock, and inner-city Dublin; and like Stephen he thought seriously about becoming a priest. There is something to be said that this essential doubleness of experience – autobiographical and fictional – is further developed in Joyce's technique of using Stephen's own way of describing and thinking about the world – his idiolect (i.e. the idiosyncratic way we all have with the language we share as birthright with others) – to inform the language of the third-person narrator. Indeed, so thoroughly are the two mixed that it is often impossible to know whether what we are reading are Stephen's own thoughts, the narrator's version of events or, in John Donne's wonderful coinage, the point at which they "intertouch". This, for example, when Stephen is lying ill in the infirmary:

> How pale the light was at the window! But that was nice. The fire rose and fell on the wall. It was like waves. Someone had put coal on and he heard voices. They were talking. It was the noise of the waves. Or the waves were talking among themselves as they rose and fell. [p. 25]

Style, then, is when language leaves the earth behind and takes flight. Like the escape from Crete of Daedalus and Icarus it is a necessity that involves risks. Fly too close to the sun – in other words develop so personal or eccentric a style as to leave the shared horizons of a common language behind – and the author risks failing to communicate the "familiar personal past" that is the writer's subject matter and the objective of their art. In these terms Stephen's voluntary exile from Ireland serves as a metaphor for every act of creative writing.

The point Barthes is making, and how it relates specifically to Joyce's use of the epiphany to expand – indeed, literally re-write – the horizons of literature in English, can also be usefully compared to Walter Benjamin's unrealised project of composing a book that was to be made entirely of quotations taken from their original context and juxtaposed with other fragments of existing texts so as to discover in each fragment a wholly new set of associations. Benjamin saw the role of the historian or writer as being one of seeing the historical moment not "as it really was" but blasted out of the continuum of history, thus liberating its full potential for revealing the contemporary crisis or danger. What is meant by this is best explained with reference to the epiphany quoted in full earlier. Read in terms of traditional historical approaches, the scene in Joyce's family home at Martello Terrace would not merit attention. History, according to such an approach, is made on the battlefield or around the treaty table. What goes on in the home, Barthes' "familiar personal past", is an irrelevance. To Benjamin and Joyce, however, it is precisely in such settings that the full impact of history is felt. As such, the mini-drama of Joyce's epiphany is seen as evidence of the dangers implicit in authority, the implied threat of some kind of physical violence, and how these give rise to guilt, shame and resentment.

In terms of the quotation, which we have already seen as a determining aspect of Stephen's 'character', Benjamin favoured the overlooked, "the 'refuse' and 'detritus' of history, the half-concealed, variegated traces of daily life of 'the collective'".[1] Clearly there are fascinating parallels here between Joyce's epiphanies and Benjamin's re-telling of history through fragments. As we will see, the parallels can be widened to take in the use of the 'throwaway' in *Ulysses* and the fragmentation and re-assemblage of the English language that is *Finnegans Wake*. For now, though, it is worth making the point that Joyce's novelistic techniques were part of an important current in European culture, one which includes the Marxist-inflected historical materialism of Benjamin, as well as more readily acknowledged movements such as the analytical cubism of Braque and Picasso, Freud's charting of the unconscious, or the atonality of Schoenberg and his disciples in the Vienna School.

That traditional artistic modes of representing the world underwent a crisis in the early decades of the 20th century is a critical commonplace, whether you believe the crisis is something to be celebrated or mourned. The reasons for this are many, but arguably one of the most coherent and influential analyses of the situation belongs to Walter Benjamin who, during the 1920s and 1930s, developed the concept of the urban phantasmagoria. According to Benjamin's theory, the city is the defining subject matter of modernist texts; a city, though, that is a theatre for dreams, fantasy and the fragmentation of memory. Clearly there are parallels here to things we have discussed in relation to *Dubliners*. And if, as Hugh Kenner imaginatively argues, every guest at the Misses Morkan's party is literally dead, then that story becomes phantasmagoric, not simply in terms of being populated by ghosts but in terms of Benjamin's use of the phrase "afterlife of works". What he meant by this, as Howard Eiland and Kevin McLaughlin explain, is that:

> Welcomed into a present moment that seems to be waiting just for it … the moment from the past comes alive as never before. In this way, the 'now' is itself experienced as preformed in the 'then' as its distillation.

Thus in 'The Dead' Gabriel experiences the 'then' of Gretta's being courted by Michael Furey as a distillation of the 'now' of their marriage. It shouldn't come as a surprise, therefore, that *A Portrait* is likewise riddled with such moments: Stephen's seeing the word 'Fœtus' carved into a desk at his father's old school and feeling "the absent students of the college about him"; Stephen's younger self appearing ghost-like, "a little boy in a grey belted suit"; the "ghostly fingers" that make his scalp tremble, and the "overcoats and waterproofs hung like gibbeted malefactors, headless and dripping and shapeless" that line the corridors of his secondary school. Each such moment is important because it marks a stage in Stephen's awakening historical conscience, an awakening that reaches a crescendo in *Ulysses* when he says "History ... is a nightmare from which I am trying to awake."

Such moments threaten and overwhelm Stephen's precarious sense of himself. Very early in the novel we see Stephen attempting to distinguish the who's-who of his world: who is mother? who is father? who is he? Later, laid up with a high temperature in the school infirmary, Stephen's personal identity and "familiar personal past" are drowned in the "familiar History" of Irish politics when he imagines himself as the dead Parnell returning from England. This fusing of Stephen's fictional biography with that of the historical Parnell is a defining feature of the novel (in *Ulysses* it will be Bloom who undergoes a similar transformation) and is a reason why Joyce had to make the now famous Christmas-dinner scene the dramatic tour-de-force that it is. Without some understanding of the destructive energies which Parnell's vertiginous rise and fall released into the Irish bloodstream we cannot fully understand the terror which grips Stephen's imagination when they present him with the "afterlife" of Parnell's actions superimposed, as it were, onto his own. Unconsciously Stephen is Parnell; and Parnell, "this man with his superb silences, his historic name, his determination, his self-control, his aloofness" as he was described by Tim Healy, is himself a kind of Daedalus/Icarus figure.

In the same way as Stephen struggles to know himself, whether at school where he writes in the flyleaf of his geography book:

Stephen Dedalus
Class of Elements
Clongowes Wood College
Sallins
County Kildare
Ireland
Europe
The World
The Universe [p. 12]

or out walking with his father, repeating over to himself

I am Stephen Dedalus. I am walking behind my father whose
name is Simon Dedalus. We are in Cork, in Ireland. Cork is a
city. Our room is in the Victoria Hotel. Victoria and Stephen
and Simon. Simon and Stephen and Victoria. Names. [p. 98]

the world and his place in it remain unstable:

The memory of his childhood suddenly grew dim. He tried to
call forth some of its vivid moments but could not. He recalled
only names: Dante, Parnell, Clane, Clongowes. A little boy
who had been taught geography ... and watched the firelight
leaping and dancing on the wall of a little bedroom in the
infirmary and dreamed of being dead ... But he had not died
then. Parnell had died ... He had not died but he had faded out
like a film in the sun. He had been lost or had wandered out of
existence for he no longer existed. [ibid]

What Stephen experiences at such moments might be termed a
kind of metaphysical vertigo, by which I mean that he is overwhelmed
by the dizzying prospects of the self in relation to the universe. Caught
between the devil of ontology, which deals with the question of how
many fundamentally distinct sorts of entities compose the universe,
and the deep blue sea of metaphysics proper, which is concerned
with describing the most general traits of reality, Stephen veers
between metaphysical abstraction ("Stephen Dedalus is my name,/
Ireland is my nation./Clongowes is my dwelling place/And heaven
my expectation.") and ontological extinction ("How strange to think
of him passing out of existence in such a way, not by death but by
fading out in the sun or by being lost and forgotten somewhere in the

44

universe."). This is crucial to the novel, and to the fulcrum of Joyce's writing: is the world knowable, and if so how is the writer to represent it?

At various stages in his development Stephen asserts that the world can be both known and articulated. Hence the flyleaf of his geography book and the varying degrees of trust he places in names to both mean and be what they signify. Hence, too, the drift of an education that teaches him that "By thinking of things you could understand them." This state of verbal security rarely lasts very long. The word "universe" on his flyleaf teases him out of thought, and "made him very tired to think that way"; and the trust he places in reason to explain things is undermined by Joyce's comic touch of having a schoolboy (the same boy who was to grow up and write *Finnegans Wake*, perhaps?) translate Julius Caesar's *Commentarii de Bello Gallico* (*Commentaries on the Gallic War*) as "*Julius Caesar wrote The Calico Belly*". For while the wor(l)d remains capable of being understood it can also can be misunderstood. And such mistranslations have a right to their own self-authorised meaning, as in the case of the word 'God':

> *Dieu* was the French for God and that was God's name too; and when anyone prayed to God and said *Dieu* then God knew at once that it was a French person that was praying. But though there were different names for God in all the different languages in the world and God understood what all the people who prayed said in their different languages still God remained always the same God and God's real name was God. [p. 13]

The young Stephen is at once fascinated and confused (fascinated because he is confused?) by the plurality of meanings which are attached to the same word:

> Suck was a queer word. The fellow called Simon Moonan that name because Simon Moonan used to tie the prefect's false sleeves behind his back and the prefect used to let on to be angry. But the sound was ugly. Once [Stephen] had washed his hands in the lavatory of the Wicklow Hotel and his father pulled the stopper up by the chain after and the dirty water went down through the hole in the basin : suck. Only louder. [p. 8]

What is also implicated in this passage is the relationship between language, authority and that 'vulgarity' which was earlier discussed with regard to Joyce's use of the epiphany. As this suggests, Joyce is not only concerned with Stephen and his own idiosyncratic relationship with language. Neither, as he gets older, is Stephen's interest quite so narrowly self-obsessive. For language in the novel also functions as another of Benjamin's phantasmagoria in which what haunts the words Stephen uses is the history of Anglo-Irish relations:

> – My ancestors threw off their language and took another, Stephen said. They allowed a handful of foreigners to subject them. Do you fancy I am going to pay in my own life and person debts they made? [p. 220]

To write in a language other than English, Stephen is saying, is not to overthrow English rule but simply to ignore it. What is needed, in Barthian terms, is a translation of the horizontal into the vertical; or what William Carlos Williams called "truth through the breakup of beautiful words". What Williams was referring to here is that Joyce's response to the English language was to destroy it in order "to let the staleness out" and to take delight in 'unEnglish'-ing it.[2] Hence Joyce's criticism of those who wanted the Irish to return to speaking Gaelic, the language of an ancestral past for which he, like Stephen, wasn't prepared to answer. It is telling that one of the characters who advocates this, Haines in *Ulysses*, is an Englishman; likewise the fact that when Haines talks in Gaelic to the woman who brings milk to the Martello Tower she is unable to respond:

> – Do you understand what he says? Stephen asked her.
> – Is it French you are talking, sir? The old woman said to Haines.
> – Irish, Buck Mulligan said. Is there Gaelic on you?
> – I thought it was Irish, she said, by the sound of it. Are you from west, sir?
> – I am an Englishman, Haines answered.
> – He's English, Buck Mulligan said, and he thinks we ought to speak Irish in Ireland.
> – Sure we ought to, the old woman said, and I'm ashamed I don't speak the language myself. I'm told it's a grand language by them that knows. [pp. 12-13]

The effect is comic, the more so when we realise that the old woman is a symbol of Ireland. Joyce's intention, however, is in deadly earnest: if the world is knowable and transcribable, it is so only in the present moment. If this means using English, so be it. For as Joyce wrote in 'A Portrait of the Artist': "these things be good which yet are corrupted".

That aesthetic considerations can re-write the world was something of which Joyce was keenly aware. Take this, for example, from Stephen's thoughts as he walks through Dublin:

> His own consciousness of language was ebbing from his brain and trickling into the very words themselves which set to band and disband themselves in wayward rhymes:
>
> > *The ivy whines upon the wall*
> > *And whines and twines upon the wall*
> > *The ivy whines upon the wall*
> > *The yellow ivy on the wall*
> > *Ivy, ivy up the wall.*
>
> Did any one ever hear such drivel? Lord Almighty! Who ever heard of ivy whining on a wall? ... The words now shone in his brain, clearer and brighter than any ivory sawn from the mottled tusks of elephants. *Ivory, ivoire, avorio, ebur.* [p. 193]

Whereas earlier in the novel Stephen has to designate both a fixed point of origin and destination for the name for God/*Dieu*, here language floats clear of the phenomenal world. In doing so, the words assume a state that approaches Walter Pater's famous comment in *Studies in the History of the Renaissance* (1873) that "All art constantly aspires towards the condition of music". I will return to this in the next chapter. For now, though, it is simply worth noting that Stephen is learning to use language apart from its inherited associations. He is, as it were, free-associating with words, allowing the sounds and rhythms an authority of their own and letting them lead him in new directions. What he is also admitting is that the same object – ivory – has a multiplicity of names, each of which will have different connotations. Language is becoming something with which Stephen plays and experiments. He is becoming a poet.

There are dangers inherent in this, dangers Joyce spelled out in his essay on Oscar Wilde and which strike us as equally applicable to Stephen Dedalus at various stages in his 'sentimental education':

> He deceived himself by thinking that he was the harbinger of the good news of neo-paganism to the suffering people. [D]eep down, if any truth is to be deduced from his subjective interpretation of Aristotle, his restless thought which proceeds by sophisms rather than syllogisms, his assimilation of other natures alien to his own, such as those of the delinquent and the humble, it is the truth inherent in the spirit of Catholicism: that man cannot reach the divine heart except across that sense of separation and loss that is called sin.

A Portrait presents us with the thoughts and sensory impressions of a single character. There is little of the realistically drawn environment of *Dubliners*. Everything that happens in the novel is there because of what it tells us about Stephen, and the novel is created from fragments of his consciousness. The other characters live in his shadow, particularly the female characters. Stephen's mother exists in a narrow world where she changes the sheets for him when he wets them as a baby, cleans his ears as a student, and puts his "new secondhand clothes in order" when he is preparing to fly Ireland. Likewise the girl who drifts in and out of the novel only so as to reflect Stephen's preposterous attitude towards women. That the girl might have a sexual identity independent of Stephen fills him with dread. At all times, then, she exists only as a cipher for his own feelings towards women: Virgin, Muse, and Scarlet Woman. Even her identity in the novel is vicarious: she is the dedicatory "To (E – C –)" of a poem he intends to write; "Emma"; "a batlike soul waking to the consciousness of itself"; and elsewhere merely "she". In this she mirrors Stephen's and Ireland's inability to fix on a clear idea of what a woman is to be. In the lack of any such model stereotypes take over, none of which are liberating. It is a determining of female role models and of men's consciousness of women to which Joyce will return in the 'Nausicaa' and 'Penelope' episodes of *Ulysses*.

While in *Dubliners* symbols and images pass from character to character, weaving their own patterns through the book as a whole (we might think of the chalice that is dropped in 'The Sisters' only to be picked up and borne "safely through a throng of foes" by the boy in 'Araby'), symbols in *A Portrait* exist so as to epiphanise the vicissitudes of Stephen's inner life. Dominant among these are the images to do with birds and flight, with blindness and sight, and with water. Though consistent in their range of meanings and terms of reference, they are used by Joyce to convey infinitely subtle modulations on the themes of the novel.

There is something to be said for the argument that in the variety of forms these sets of images assume, and in the imaginative hoops through which Joyce trains them, they become analogous to the gods and mortals of Ovid's *Metamorphoses* whom we see appearing in various guises: human, animal, vegetable, and mineral. Certainly it is this aspect of the novel's construction that draws attention away from Stephen and towards the underlying forces that are shaping him. For instance, in just the first section of Chapter One water appears as the sheets Stephen wets, his mother's tears as she waves him away to school, as dirty water emptied down a sink, as cocoa and tea, the ditch into which Stephen is pushed, rain, the sweat on Stephen's forehead, and the sea over which Parnell's body is borne home to Ireland for burial. Likewise, the novel's use of bird imagery encompasses such diverse experiences as playing football ("the greasy leather orb flew like a heavy bird through the grey light"), Christmas dinner ("the plump turkey which had lain, trussed and skewered, on the kitchen table"), Stephen's fear of his teachers ("[his] heart was beating and fluttering"), the names of Stephen's friends (Heron, Cran[e]ly), and most tellingly of all the girl Stephen watches bathing in the sea and who seems the apotheosis of all that is Ovidian and expressively erotic in the novel ("She seemed like one whom magic had changed into the likeness of a strange and beautiful seabird. ... Her thighs, fuller and softhued as ivory, were bared almost to the hips where the white fringes of her drawers were like featherings of soft white down.").

Joyce's use of symbols in the novel touches on a fascinating aspect of Carl Kerényi's disquisition on myth in a book on which he collaborated with the psychologist Jung.[3] Quoting from Bronislaw Malinowski's *Myth in Primitive Psychology*, in which Malinowski says that "The myth in a primitive society ... is not a mere tale told but a reality lived ... through which the present life, fate, and work of mankind are governed", Kerényi goes on to further analyse the function of myths:

> Mythology gives a ground, lays a foundation. It does not
> answer the question 'Why?' but 'whence?' ... Mythology does
> not actually indicate 'causes' [which for] the earliest Greek
> philosophers ... were, for instance, water, fire, or what they
> called ... the 'Boundless'. No mere 'causes', therefore, but
> primary substances or primary states that never age, can never
> be surpassed, and produce everything always.

Considered in this light, we can see how Joyce uses symbols such as
water or birds in a way that would have been familiar to the Greeks.
Such symbols do not offer any single answer as to why Stephen acts
the way he does, they simply point towards the origin of his actions
in a way analogous to the 'whence' of his Christian-Hellenic name.
Stephen thus becomes, in Kerényi's terms, the archetypal "artist,
creator, founder" who "draw their strength from and build on that
source whence the mythologies have their ultimate ground and
origin". Just as such myths are anterior to the life of the individual,
so too the elemental forces of water and flight in the novel exist as
both a part of, and apart from, Stephen's developing consciousness
of himself.

From whence Stephen comes, of course, is language. The novel,
remember, starts not with his birth but with the moment at which he
becomes aware of language as both external to, yet defining his sense
of, identity. That the opening of the novel has a fairy-tale-like feel to
it means that it conforms to another aspect of Kerényi's argument,
namely that mythology stands outside the governance of biography,
even when dealing with the birth of a god:

> If anyone supposes that, in the child god, he has discovered
> the biographical element of mythology, he is heading for
> surprises. For here, at this seemingly biographical point, he
> will find himself completely outside all biography and in the
> primordial realm of mythology where the most marvellous
> creations grow and flourish.

Stephen Dedalus, then, exists only in so much as he is the point at
which we see before us the interaction of 'causes'. That these 'causes'
are capable of multiple interpretations, or of taking on aspects over
which Stephen has only the most fleeting control, is only natural.
For as Jung writes in response to Kerényi's essay 'The Primordial

Child in Primordial Times':

> The archetype does not proceed from physical facts, but
> describes how the psyche experiences the physical fact, and
> in so doing the psyche often behaves so autocratically that it
> denies tangible reality or makes statements that fly in the face
> of it.

Thus 'Stephen', a character in a novel, is simply the latest incarnation
of those archetypes that include Daedalus, Icarus, Lucifer and St
Stephen. His quest, to put it that way, is to fly in the face of those
aspects of reality – nets thrown to hold the Irish soul – these figures
represent.

That Joyce both embraced and rejected these archetypes is what
gives the novel its dynamic tension. They function, as it were, as a
meniscus: providing both a boundary and an elasticity to Joyce's
material. As the artist who fashions a work of art from pre-existing
material, he is like Kerényi's model of the teller of myths who "steps
back into primordiality ["Once upon a time and a very good time it
was"] in order to tell us what 'originally was'". What Joyce comes
back with, however, is the knowledge that as humans we cannot go
any further back than the moment of our 'baptism' in language (for
the inroads Joyce made into the preconscious we will have to wait
until *Finnegans Wake*), and that our understanding of the world is
bounded by our ability to contain it in words: "What was after the
universe? Nothing. But was there anything round the universe to
show where it stopped before the nothing place began?" Even myth,
which Jung calls "revelations of the preconscious psyche" will only
take us so far: "The ultimate core of meaning may be circumscribed,
but not described". And with this we return to Joyce's use of water
and birds which, to continue with Jung's model, "circumscribe and
give an approximate description of an *unconscious core of meaning.*
The ultimate meaning of this nucleus was never conscious and never
will be. It was, and still is, only interpreted". This "unconscious core
of meaning", of course, belongs solely to Stephen in the novel until,
that is, he recognises that how he interprets experience is determined
by his belonging to a particular 'race' or, to use a contemporary term,
a specific 'interpretative community'. After this he must acknowledge
that his ability to know the world is necessarily circumscribed if he

is to avoid the fate of Icarus and Lucifer. The artist, Joyce is saying, must accept both the given *and* the necessity of re-fashioning it, as he does the events of his own life in this his fictionalised autobiography. Thus two ways of knowing the world and our part in it are opened up for exploration: the facts, and the connotations of those facts when immersed in language, or the symbolic. The final irony, however, and it is one which leaves us fearful for Stephen's ultimate success, is that at the very point of preparing to fly Ireland he returns to childhood and myth, remaining reliant on his mother to put his "new secondhand clothes in order" and on Daedalus – "Old father, old artificer, stand me now and ever in good stead" – to provide parental guidance. At the end, then, Stephen, consciously or not, assumes the role of Icarus. Pride, it seems, has ascendancy over "silence, exile and cunning".

While we might argue that *Dubliners* is suspended in the aspic of its own objectivity, *A Portrait* struggles with the fierceness of its essential subjectivity. That it accomplishes this so brilliantly shouldn't blind us to the fact that by limiting itself to the sensibility of a boy who is hardly out of adolescence when the novel ends, Joyce is providing us with an experience of reading a novel that at one and the same time allows us to approve and disapprove of Stephen's actions and his world view. The novel marks a progression in Joyce's stated aim of writing "a moral history" of Ireland. Part of this moral, however, is to criticise that process of liberation or self-completion which is the artist's goal. The labyrinth from which Daedalus escapes, we remember, was fashioned by himself. There is, then, something essentially tragic about *A Portrait*, as though at the conclusion Stephen becomes a version of the blinded Oedipus setting out into exile alone. If this isn't an image that springs readily to mind when we think of Joyce's work as a whole, that is due to *Ulysses* and the world of Rabelaisian appetite and excess which it reintroduced to 20th century literature.

Footnotes

[1] Walter Benjamin, *The Arcades Project,* Translated by Howard Eiland and Kevin McLaughlin (The Belnap Press: Cambridge, Massachusetts, and London, England, 1999).

² 'A Note on the Recent Work of James Joyce' (1927), *Selected Essays of William Carlos Williams*, pp. 75-79.

³ *The Science of Mythology: Essays on the Myth of the Divine Child and the Mysteries of Eleusis* (1941) by C.G. Jung and C. Kerényi (Routledge: London and New York, 1985). For a spell Lucia Joyce was a patient of Jung's; and in 1932 Jung wrote an article on *Ulysses* which, in a letter to Joyce, he called "an exceedingly hard nut to crack [but which] I learned a great deal from".

4

Changing the Subject: *Ulysses*

When, in 1922, T.S. Eliot wrote that Joyce's use of Homer's *Odyssey* to underpin his own modern epic "made the modern world possible for art" he was able to assume that readers of *Ulysses* both recognised that the title was the Latin form of the name Odysseus and that the parallels between the novel and Homer's poem would be understood. As Jennifer Levin has usefully commented, this isn't necessarily the case today when the name 'Ulysses' has shed its older associations and now "seems entirely Joycean". To regain something of the frisson Joyce's title originally caused, we need, she suggests, to "Imagine for a moment that this seven hundred page novel is called *Hamlet* and you will regain a sense of it as a text brought into deliberate collision with a powerful predecessor."[1]

Edmund Wilson's essay on Joyce, first published in *Axel's Castle* in 1931, remains a model of lucidity and first-time readers of *Ulysses* can do worse than to read Wilson for his command of both the novel's architectonics plus his insights into some finer details. I quote him here at some length so as to provide the unfamiliar reader with a synopsis of both the *Odyssey* and *Ulysses*, and to hear what Wilson had to say about the connections between them:

> The key to 'Ulysses' is in the title – and this key is indispensable if we are to appreciate the book's real depth and scope. Ulysses, as he figures in the 'Odyssey', is a sort of type of the average intelligent Greek: among the heroes he is distinguished for cunning rather than exalted wisdom, and for common sense, quickness and nerve [.] The 'Odyssey' exhibits such a man in practically every situation and relation of an ordinary human life – Ulysses, in the course of his wanderings, runs the whole gauntlet of temptations and ordeals and through his wits he

survives them all to return at last to his home and family and to reassert himself there as master. ... Now the 'Ulysses' of Joyce is a modern 'Odyssey' in both subject and form; and the significance of the characters and incidents of its ostensibly Naturalistic narrative cannot properly be understood without reference to the Homeric original. Joyce's Telemachus ... is Stephen Dedalus [and] we have seen him, at the end of [*A Portrait*,] on the point of leaving for France to study and write. ... Stephen has announced at the end of the earlier book that he is going forth to 'forge in the smithy of my soul the uncreated conscience of my race'; and now he has returned to Dublin baffled and disinherited – his life with [Buck] Mulligan is dissolute and unproductive. ... Ulysses is a Dublin Jew, an advertisement canvasser named Bloom. Like Stephen, he dwells among aliens: a Jew and the son of a Hungarian father, he is still more or less of a foreigner among the Irish ... He has been married for sixteen years to the buxom daughter of an Irish army officer, a professional singer, of prodigious sexual appetite [.] They have one daughter [and] one son, of whom Bloom had hoped that he might resemble, that he might refine upon, himself, but who died eleven days after he was born ... He is aware that his wife has lovers; but he does not complain or try to interfere [.] He is a Ulysses with no Telemachus and cut off from his Penelope.

Joyce rightly guessed that his novel would bamboozle many readers, and from the off he did everything he could to aid understanding of the work. It had been agreed that at the novel's launch on 7th December 1921 Valery Larbaud, the acclaimed French novelist and poet, would give an introductory talk about *Ulysses*, and so in early November Joyce sent him a copy of an intricate schema which showed its Homeric parallels. This same schema had been sent by Joyce in 1920 to Carlo Linati, the Italian translator of *Exiles*. In the accompanying letter Joyce outlined to Linati other aspects of *Ulysses*:

> It is the epic of two races (Israel-Ireland) and at the same time the cycle of the human body as well as a little story of a day (life). The character of Ulysses has fascinated me ever since boyhood. I started writing a short story for *Dubliners* fifteen years ago but gave it up. For seven years I have been working at this book – blast it! It is also a kind of encyclopaedia.

When the novel was finally published it was divided into three numbered chapters, with each chapter containing a number of episodes. Thus the first three episodes make up the *Telemachia* (the story of Telemachus' search for his lost father, Odysseus); the next 12 the *Odyssey* proper (telling of Odysseus' wanderings on his ten-year journey home from the Trojan war); and the final three the *Nostos* (or 'return home', where Odysseus is reunited both with Telemachus and Penelope, his wife). As the Linati schema makes clear, each of the novel's 18 episodes contained further Homeric parallels: thus the *Telemachia* comprises 'Telemachus', 'Nestor' and 'Proteus'; the *Odyssey* 'Calypso', 'Lotus Eaters', 'Hades', 'Aeolus', 'Lestrygonians', 'Scylla and Charybdis', 'Wandering Rocks', 'Sirens', 'Cyclops', 'Nausicaa', 'Oxen of the Sun', and 'Circe'; and the *Nostos* rounds off the novel with 'Eumaeus', 'Ithaca' and 'Penelope'.

While there is no doubt that some understanding of the Homeric parallels can aid understanding of *Ulysses*, it is useful to balance this against Hugh Kenner's comment that "Before rushing to embrace it as an … antidote to all mysteries, the reader should reflect that the object of reading the book is not to reconstruct the schema, any more than one eats a dinner to reconstruct the recipes. It is not a set of answers to a puzzle". This is sound advice, as is Jennifer Levine's comment that "While long sections of surrounding text may remain opaque, a single page, or paragraph, or even a few lines can generate enough of a sense that it does all work out … to keep us going". Though not always easy going, *Ulysses* is never dull (having said this, *The Oxen of the Sun* episode, for all its virtuosity comes, like Liszt, perilously close). And though it frequently eludes an easily summarisable 'meaning', Levine is spot-on in saying that suddenly, among a welter of confused impressions, the reader is rewarded by a paragraph or a phrase of crystalline prose that lights up the surrounding text. It is for this that we persevere with reading *Ulysses* in the first place, and why we return to it again and again.

Ulysses had been Joyce's favourite hero as a schoolboy, and he wrote an essay on him while at Belvedere. A story called 'Ulysses' that would have described the peregrinations of a man called Hunter was planned for inclusion in *Dubliners* but "never got any forrarder than the title". Indeed, at one point Joyce even considered calling his book of short stories *Ulysses at Dublin*. This, then, is simply to say that *Ulysses* was not unique in Joyce's output in having Homer in mind. It's just that in *Ulysses* he wanted it to be brought to the fore of the reader's imagination. Why?

One answer to this is suggested by Kenner's observation that Homer's *Odyssey* is present so as to provide a scaffolding:

> [Joyce] was building (was he not?) an ordered book out of chaos, and needed a plan. It was only after the image of artist as imposer of order, lawgiver to his limp materials, had been lived to the dregs and discarded ... that he could understand with his whole mind how Homer could control the *treatment* of Dublin material because it illuminated the *subject*.

This returns us to an aspect of what I had earlier to say about *A Portrait*, namely that in as much as the artist fashions a work of art from pre-existing material, he is like Kerényi's model of the teller of myths who "steps back into primordiality" in order to tell us what "originally was". Kerényi, however, provides another model for the writer – the philosopher who "tries to pierce through the world of appearance in order to say what 'really is'". This brings us close to something Edmund Wilson had to say about Joyce: that in spite of the "nervous intensity" of *Ulysses*, "we are in the presence of a mind which has much in common with that of a certain type of philosopher, who in his effort to understand the causes of things, to interrelate the different elements of the universe, has reached a point where the ordinary values of good and bad, beautiful and ugly, have been lost in the excellence and beauty of transcendent understanding itself."

Homer, then, allowed Joyce access to the 'primordial' or those 'causes' which in *A Portrait* are represented by certain key symbols, while also providing a degree of objectivity from the historical causes and effects which blight both the individual and collective lives of characters in *Dubliners*. Thus in *Ulysses* the basic analogies between Homeric Greece and 20th-century Dublin are reasonably clear: Ireland is Ithaca; England is Poseidon (Odysseus' enemy at sea); and the quest for the father is, in Kenner's words, "the quest for the rational and masculine". There is another level of such correspondences, often used for comic or satiric effect. For example: Bloom's "knockmedown cigar" is the sharpened, red-hot club used to blind the Cyclops, who himself corresponds with the bigoted Irish Nationalist, the Citizen. Such correspondences, however, refer to the past. Inasmuch as he wanted his novel to speak of, and for, modern Dublin, what Kerényi calls "what 'really is'" rather than "what 'originally was'", Joyce allows discrepancies to appear. Thus his Penelope isn't faithful, Stephen isn't Bloom's son, Nausicaa (Gerty MacDowell) doesn't take Bloom home with her to meet her father, and Bloom doesn't slaughter Molly's 'suitor' (Blazes Boylan). The reader who looks only for direct parallels will, as T.S. Eliot saw, easily become confused:

> We need an eye which can see the past in its place with its definite differences from the present, and yet so lively that it shall be as present to us as the present. This is the creative eye[.]

This is not to say that we can make sense of Joyce by shoehorning him into one or other of Kerényi's models. Not without running the risk of losing something vital – the essential modernity of *Ulysses*. Bloom isn't Ulysses, nor was he meant to be. The hero of the Hellenic myths, as W.H. Auden wrote, was "responsible neither for his successes nor his failures. When Odysseus succeeds, he has Pallas Athena to thank; when he fails, he has Poseidon to blame." The fact is that no such divine assistance or hindrance is available to Stephen, Bloom or Molly. Their successes or failures are to be judged in human terms. If this makes them lesser heroes, so be it; for it also means that Bloom, rather than slaughtering his rival, simply clambers into bed and brushes away the remains of his presence. Should he kill him, he thinks? Never, "as two wrongs did not make it right." We might all prefer to be Odysseus, Telemachus or Penelope. The truth is that most of us would end up as one of Odysseus' hapless crew members, or one of Nausicaa's maids or the chancers who live off the fat of Ithaca while laying siege to Penelope's bedroom. These are the characters the gods choose to overlook. In other words, they are us.

Joyce was a solitary writer. He abhorred dogma and ideology, and though he could be garrulous in company he tended to avoid political argument. This is not the same as saying that he was apolitical, as is shown by even the most cursory reading of the nine articles he wrote on Irish themes for publication in the Triestine newspaper *Il Piccolo della Sera* between 1907-1912.[2] Joyce desired and was committed to Irish independence as much as the most hardline nationalist – we might say even more so, given the symbiotic relationship Joyce saw as existing between Nationalism and Imperialism – it was just that he was not prepared to engage in the same tactics. He was a committed supporter of Sinn Féin – "Either Sinn Féin or Imperialism will conquer the present Ireland" – though he would have been appalled at the violence adopted by some 'Shinners' following Independence and the ensuing Civil War. What Joyce was acutely sensitive to is a point of view that has been brilliantly analysed by the Lebanese-born, French-speaking novelist Amin Maalouf:

> The fact is, it's difficult to say where legitimate affirmation of identity ends and encroachment on the rights of others begins. … It starts by reflecting a perfectly permissible aspiration, then before we know where we are it has become an instrument of war. The transition from one meaning to the other is imperceptible, almost natural, and sometimes we all just go along with it. We are denouncing an injustice, we are defending the rights of a suffering people – then the next day we find ourselves accomplices in a massacre.[3]

Given this, and given Joyce's internationalist sympathies we shouldn't be surprised to discover that he was also a socialist. In part it was Socialism that lay behind 'A Portrait of the Artist' with its rousing call to the working-classes, and where the mention of "the general paralysis of an insane society" offers an interesting angle on what was to follow in *Dubliners*:

> Man and woman, out of you comes the nation that is to come, the lightening of your masses in travail. The competitive order is employed against you, the aristocracies are supplanted; and amid the general paralysis of an insane society, the confederate will issues in action.

Elsewhere Joyce's socialism was expressed in more considered if no less passionate fashion. Take this from another letter to Stanislaus:

> You have often shown opposition to my socialistic tendencies. But can you not see plainly from facts like these that a

cracked mirror signifies Joyce's foregrounding of the means by which things are represented. If, for example, one aspect of literary naturalism is that, to paraphrase Hamlet, it holds a mirror up to nature in such a way as to blind us to the fact that what we are reading is an artifice, Joyce never allows the reader to settle into any such illusion. Rather he wants us to be aware that the artistic representation of reality is essentially determined and defined by discourse. Hence the shifts in the novel between interior monologue, omniscient narrator, drama, parody, satire, etc. To give a further example: in a famous photograph of Paris by the Hungarian photographer André Kertész our unmediated view of the city is disrupted by the fact that the image is punctuated by a bullet-hole-like fracture, the result of the glass plate negative having been broken. The effect, as with Joyce's use of different styles, is to shift the reader's attention away from the subject matter and towards the means of representation. The crack in the mirror forces Stephen to become self-conscience. Likewise the reader.

A further development of the techniques of *A Portrait* is the complex patterning of symbols that run throughout the novel, many of which have their origins in the opening episode. Thus we encounter a tower, a feline creature (Haines' nightmarish panther), green gems (Haines' silver cigarette case "in which twinkled a green stone"), and a woman delivering milk. Unlike *A Portrait*, however, the symbols are not determined solely in relation to Stephen. Thus in 'Calypso', the episode in which we are first introduced to Leopold Bloom, the tower becomes Bloom himself while he is giving a saucer of milk to a green-eyed cat.

'Nestor'

In *A Portrait* we have witnessed Stephen as both schoolboy and undergraduate. Now we see him as a schoolteacher teaching history in a private boy's school in Dalkey. The school is owned and run by Mr Deasy, an anti-Semitic, pro-British Ulster Scot who tells Stephen that an Englishman's proudest boast is "I paid my way." Stephen, it goes without saying, is unable to say the same. In 'Telemachus' we have been told that it is he and not Mulligan who pays the rent on the Martello Tower, and that Mulligan is relying on Stephen's pay from the school for the drinking session he has planned for later that day.

Throughout the novel Joyce is at pains not to spare the reader from the economic realities of his characters and the various debts they incur as the day progresses. While Stephen is teaching the boys ancient history, his mind keeps returning to more recent historical events: William of Orange; the massacre of Catholic tenants in Armagh; and the 'croppy boy', a song which makes reference to the 1798 Rebellion and to which Joyce returns throughout the novel. Little wonder Stephen tells Mr Deasy that "History ... is a nightmare from which I am trying to awake." Stephen also has the boys recite lines from 'Lycidas', Milton's elegy for a drowned friend, and which parallels the body of the man "that was drowned nine days ago off Maiden's Rock" and whose body has yet to be found. Both cannot fail to have troubling connotations for Stephen given his continuing doubts as to whether he is Daedalus or Icarus.

'Proteus'

The first episode in which interior monologue dominates. The importance of what happens in this episode, then, is contained in the drama of Stephen's thoughts.

Proteus was an ancient sea god with whom King Menelaus wrestled on the seashore. In Homer's *Odyssey*, Proteus is able to change form at will, able to assume "the shape of every creature that moves on earth, and of water and of portentous fire". To catch hold of him, then, is not easy. Thus in this episode Stephen's thoughts are continually changing shape and direction as he walks, thinks, sits, urinates, writes a poem and picks his nose on Sandymount Strand. The use of interior monologue also allows us to judge the distance that has grown up between the 'Stephen' of *A Portrait* and the 'Stephen' of *Ulysses*.

The essential instability of language as it refers to things can be found throughout the episode. Stephen's hat, for example, is called "My Latin quarter hat", a "cockle hat and staff" and later "my Hamlet hat". Stephen is aware too of change being an essential component of life and death: "God becomes man becomes fish becomes barnacle goose becomes featherbed mountain." Once again, Joyce is drawing our attention to the metaphorical and to the unconscious processes of association.

Events such as seeing two midwives, a dead dog being sniffed at by a living dog, a man and a woman picking cockles and a ship sailing out to sea, lead Stephen to thinking about 14th-century Dublin, 16th century Denmark, and 17th-century London; to memories of his recent stay in Paris, his own adolescent writings, and to acting out the role of Hamlet. Stephen's mind is a bricollage of other texts: Aristotle, Jakob Boehme, Dante, William Blake, Thomas Aquinas and Shakespeare to name just a few. As such, it is true to say that Stephen does not exist apart from those things that he has read and written about. He is also, as he is only too aware, the product of more familiar influences:

> Wombed in sin darkness I was too, made not begotten. By them, the man with my voice and my eyes and a ghostwoman with ashes on her breath. They clasped and sundered, did the coupler's will. [p. 73]

To argue that there is a Stephen distinct from his influences is, on the basis of this episode, impossible. The world for Stephen exists as text: "Signatures of all things I am here to read, seaspawn and seawrack, the nearing tide, that rusty boot. Snotgreen, bluesilver, rust: coloured signs." In addition to this he is acutely sensitive to whether or not he is himself being observed: "Who ever anywhere will read these written words? Signs on a white field"; "Can't see! Who's behind me?"; "Behind. Perhaps there is someone." Is this Stephen's guilt over his mother's death, his shame at his family's diminished reputation, or is he conscious of the reader looking over his shoulder?

'Calypso'

Having left Stephen "walking into eternity along Sandymount strand" at sometime approaching midday, the narrative backtracks and returns the reader to eight o'clock that same morning and the altogether earthly abode of 7 Eccles Street, the residence of Leopold and Marion ('Molly') Bloom. Thus the timescale of this and the following two episodes parallels that of the first three. As we have seen in relation to Joyce's use of symbols other patterns are repeated, though with different emphasis. Bloom is immediately contrasted with Stephen: his "relish[ing] the inner organs of beasts and fowls" counterpointing

Stephen's shrinking from "the urinous offal from all dead". In general terms, Bloom celebrates the body while Stephen is repelled by it; and while Stephen is all quivering sensitivity and intellectual prowess, Bloom is much more straight-forward and commonsensical. He is a comic (in the Aristotelian sense of the word) Everyman for whom knowledge of himself and the world has not come about through any lack of suffering: his Jewish, Hungarian-born father killed himself, and his only son, Rudy, died aged 11 days.

Given what we know about Joyce's refusal to assign human behaviour to simplistic binary oppositions we should not expect the characters of Stephen and Bloom to so simplistically arrange themselves. Most tellingly, of course, this first episode involving Bloom shares the interior monologue that we have come to associate solely with Stephen. Rather than viewing them as polar opposites, then, we are better to judge Bloom and Stephen as 'Contraries'. Like Stephen, Bloom moves through his world interpreting the signs as he goes: the cat's behaviour means that she is hungry and needs milk, and he is able to successfully translate Molly's "Mn" in answer to his asking her if she wants any breakfast as "No". Again like Stephen he is distrustful about the ultimate stability of textual representations of life: "Probably not a bit like it really. Kind of stuff you read". In this they are both like Molly who, in her great monologue at the novel's close, declares that "I dont like books with a Molly in them" and "theres nothing for a woman in that all invention made up". In this Joyce is grounding his novel in a certain self-reflexivity, granting it the ability to comment on its own processes and to questions its claims to truth-making.

In terms of the Homeric parallels, Bloom/Ulysses is surrounded by a bevy of nymphs including Molly, his daughter Milly, the girl next door, the cat, and the bathing nymphs in the picture over his and Molly's bed and into which, at four o'clock that afternoon, she will invite Blazes Boylan. Stephen and Bloom are similar in one other important way: they will both spend the day wandering through Dublin disinherited and unable to return home. Ireland is implicitly also lost and disinherited, as shown by Bloom's musings on Irish Nationalism and the Home Rule movement. The irony, not wasted on Bloom who, like every good sailor, can navigate by the sun and stars, is that the headpiece of *The Freeman's Journal* shows "a homerule sun rising up in the northwest from the laneway behind the bank of Ireland". Economic matters, too, are a governing aspect of Bloom's day – from adding up the price of sausages to looking after the little that remains of Stephen's pay when they finally meet that evening.

'Lotus Eaters'

Here further aspects of the general paralysis examined in *Dubliners* come into play. In Homeric terms the Lotus Eaters were the inhabitants of an island who, once having tasted the lotus flowers, were disinclined ever to leave. Joyce equates the lotus, among other things, with the Eucharist; its verbal equivalent being the Latin of the Catholic Mass. These references are underscored by the fact that the episode sees Bloom collecting from the post office a letter from 'Martha Clifford' with whom, under the nom de plume of 'Henry Flower' he is carrying on a libidinous, though ultimately vicarious, correspondence. As Jeri Johnson says:

> Numbness and stupefaction, libidinal and mental narcosis, are close correlatives in Lotus Eaters where the effects of 'lotus' can be located in the gelded cabhorses, the potion of Sweeney the chemist, 'Lovephiltres' or the 'Lourdes cure, waters of oblivion.'

The maintainers of this state are everywhere to be seen: the recruiting posters for the British army pinned up in the post office, and the notice on the church door of All Hallows advertising a sermon by "the very reverend John Conmee S.J. on saint Peter Claver S.J. and the African mission." As in *A Portrait*, where saint Francis Xavier, the patron of Stephen's college, is linked with the colonisation of Africa, India, Japan and China, the Church is here further linked with oppression. Other associations enter Bloom's mind when looking at the recruiting advert:

> Maud Gonne's letter about taking them off O'Connell Street at night: disgrace to our Irish capital. [A]n army rotten with venereal disease: overseas or halfseasover empire. Half baked they look: hypnotised like. Eyes front. Mark time. [p. 59]

The letter to which Bloom is referring was in fact a pamphlet, ostensibly written by Gonne, during the Boer War (1899-1902) when British troops in Dublin were not confined to barracks at night and were accused of creating a nuisance. The Boer War is, for Bloom, a touchstone of Anglo-Irish relations, focusing as it did much moderate Irish opinion into a more radical anti-Imperialism. The letter also serves to anticipate Stephen's run-in with two British soldiers in 'Circe', and the connections between Empire and sexually transmitted disease that is one of the themes of that episode.

'Hades'

In the *Odyssey*, Circe tells Odysseus that before continuing on his journey home to Ithaca he must visit the underworld in order to consult with the dead. There Odysseus meets with one of his own dead sailors, the prophet Tiresias who warns him that his voyage home will not be easily achieved, Achilles, and the ghost of his own mother who has died while awaiting his return. For Bloom the events surrounding the funeral of Paddy Dignam are no less psychologically arduous. Forced by his companions to confront aspects of his own past, notably his father's death by suicide, he is also left to mourn the death of his only son and the subsequent sterility of his marriage. Bloom is also haunted by the feeling of being out of place in Dublin, a fact brought home by the frequently vicious and unthinkingly anti-Semitic comments of the other funeral goers, and the sighting of Blazes Boylan which leads to innuendoes about the relationship between Boylan and Molly. Ireland's past also threatens to overwhelm him and the other funeral goers: they discuss Ben Dollard's rendition of 'The Croppy Boy'; the cortège passes the statue of Daniel O'Connell, "the hugecloaked Liberator's form", and the statue of Nelson in Sackville Street. After the funeral a group of men go to visit Parnell's grave:

> They turned to the right, following their slow thoughts. With awe Mr Power's blank voice spoke:
> – Some say he is not in that grave at all. That the coffin was filled with stones. That one day he will come again. [pp. 92-3]

Bloom does not join them. Refusing to allow his thoughts to stay among the dead, he casts a cold eye on the grave stones and monuments, "old Ireland's hearts and hands", asserting that it would be

"More sensible to spend the money on some charity for the living." Ultimately it is Bloom's affirmation of life, of the heart, that enables him to banish the gathering ghosts.

'Aeolus'

Aeolus gave Odysseus a bag containing all the winds unnecessary to his safe crossing home to Ithaca. Convinced that it contained a treasure that Odysseus was keeping secret from them, his sailors undid the bag and released the winds. The ship was blown back out to sea and their homecoming was further delayed. In terms of *Ulysses*, the winds are replaced by another kind of hot air: rhetoric. Set in the shared offices of the *Freeman's Journal* (the newspaper whose commitment to Home Rule has been commented on earlier) and the *Evening Telegraph*, journalists, newspaper talk and the mechanical processes of the printing presses abound. References to famous Greek and Irish orators sit alongside the sounds of the presses, the "Thump, thump, thump" and "Sllt" of the mechanised production of words. What the voice of the presses also introduces, of course, is the sound of technological process, of a time that is to do with neither human biology nor consciousness. It is, as Steven Connor usefully puts it, "the intersection of language and social life, or the wordy and worldly." These voices are not limited to the newspaper offices: "Before Nelson's pillar trams slowed, shunted, changed trolley … clanging, ringing". For the first time, then, we are given a sense of Dublin as a mechanism rather than a place of culture.

That the chapter has been deliberately, and not a little ironically arranged is immediately clear from the Headlines that punctuate the text. This editorial hand is distinct from the narrator. Not only do the headlines fragment the text but they encourage us to read against the grain what is being narrated. In short, they serve to undermine the self-important posturings of the newspapermen.

Not surprisingly given the surroundings, references to Britain and Ireland abound. The English language is compared unfavourably by Professor MacHugh (who is unconsciously echoing Mr Deasy) to Greek: "I speak the tongue of a race the acme of whose mentality is the maxim: time is money … The closetmaker and the cloacamaker will never be lords of our spirit." While this is going on Bloom is busy putting together an advert for Alexander Keyes, tea, wine and spirit merchant. The point of the ad is that it will be a visual pun on the word 'Keys', as in the House of Keys, the lower house of the Manx Parliament, the Isle of Man being independent of the British Parliament and therefore an allusion to Irish Home Rule. The point, of course, is that advertising can be effective means of ideological discourse: while what is ostensibly being advertised is tea and wine, the wider implications of the image that accompanies the text is directed at a receptive reader. Elsewhere in the episode Stephen seeks to ingratiate himself with the newspaper men by telling the story of Anne Kearns and Florence MacCabe, "Two Dublin vestals" who climb to the top of Nelson's pillar only to arrive at the summit "too tired to look up or down or to speak." The story, which reads like an offcut from *Dubliners*, meets with success, the men recognising in it a parable of Irish ambitions for independence.

'Lestrygonians'

As Hugh Kenner notes, the imagery now shifts from mechanism to cannibalism. The time is 1.00pm and Bloom is hungry. Unfortunately his efforts at finding somewhere to eat lunch are frustrated by his disgust at his fellow-Dubliners' eating habits and his musings about the wider economic, religious and political connotations and implications of food production.

The Homeric parallel is Odysseus' encounter with the cannibalistic King Antiphates, a parallel Joyce develops to include references to Christ's sacrificial death ("Blood of the Lamb", "God wants blood victim."), the monarchy ("His Majesty the king. God. Save. Our. Sitting on his throne sucking red jujubes white."), the social costs of the Catholic Church outlawing birth control ("Increase and multiply. Did you ever hear such an idea? Eat you out of house and home."), religion and Anglo-Irish relations ("They say they used to give pauper children soup to change to protestants in the time of the potato blight."), and the economic cost of Ireland having to export her best produce to Britain. This is a theme that runs throughout the novel and is a cause of Irish resentment. In 'Nestor' we have heard extracts from an angry article on cattle exports and foot-and-mouth disease that Mr Deasy wants Stephen to use his influence and help have published in one of the Dublin newspapers; now we have Bloom recollecting how such anger can take other forms – notably the pro-

Boer demonstrations of 1899:

> – Up the Boers!
> – Three cheers for De Wet!
> – We'll hang Joe Chamberlain on a sourapple tree. [p. 133]

The pacifist and socialist in Bloom is saddened by such events. He is also angry at the ways in which prices are kept artificially high, and that what people are prepared to eat is swayed by the vagaries of fashion and class:

> Half the catch of oysters they throw back in the sea to keep up the price. Cheap no-one would buy. Caviare. Do the grand. Hock in green glasses. Swell blowout. Lady this. Powdered bosom pearls. The *élite*. *Crème de la crème*. [p. 143]

Watching the diners in the Burton restaurant leads Bloom to a wide-ranging conclusion: "Every fellow for his own, tooth and nail. Gulp. Grub. Gulp. Gobstuff ... Eat or be eaten. Kill! Kill!" That Bloom is unconsciously echoing the poet laureate Tennyson's famous lines about nature being red in tooth and claw only re-focuses our attention on the relationship between Ireland and Britain as essentially cannibalistic.

'Scylla and Charybdis'

Caught between the Devil and the deep blue sea, a rock and a hard place, the frying pan or the fire, it is now 2.00pm and Stephen is in the National Library in Kildare Street arguing about the 'facts' of Shakespeare's life and their relationship to his art with George Russell (who wrote under the pseudonym, 'AE') and W.K. Magee (who wrote essays modelled on Matthew Arnold's graceful style under the name 'John Eglinton', and as co-editor of *Dana* rejected Joyce's 'A Portrait of the Artist'). The Scylla and Charybdis (the rocks or whirlpool past which Odysseus must choose which way to sail) of the debate are whether the artist creates his work out of "ideas, formless spiritual essences" or, as Stephen counters, the imaginative transformation (or transubstantiation) of history: "Space: what you damn well have to see", "the now, the here, through which all future plunges to the past." The debate centres on Shakespeare as the 'national poet':

" – Our Irish bards, John Eglinton censured, have yet to create a figure which the world will set beside Saxon Shakespeare's Hamlet". With wonderful irony, Stephen, wearing as he is his "Hamlet hat", is Joyce's deliberate rebuttal of this claim. Likewise, the claims of literature to float clear of history are dealt a blow by Stephen's reading of the character of Hamlet in light of British military tactics during the Boer war: "Khaki Hamlets don't hesitate to shoot. The bloodboltered shambles in act five is a forecast of the concentration camp". What we also have is an anticipation of one reason Joyce refuses to have Bloom respond with violence to Molly's having been unfaithful. All aggression, the novel asserts, is tied up with empire and conquest.

The episode also sees an interesting development in the theme of father/son relations, with Stephen's aesthetic theories suggesting that the artist must become his own father in that he must revisit the facts of his life and reconfigure them through the "conscious begetting" of the work of art. As such the artist unmakes history and fashions it in his own image:

> When [Shakespeare] wrote *Hamlet* he was not the father of
> his own son merely but, being no more than a son, he was
> and felt himself the father of all his race, the father of his
> own grandfather, the father of his unborn grandson. [p. 171]

As always with Stephen, his thoughts are never far from the uncertainties of his own name and identity: "Fabulous artificer. The hawklike man. You flew. Whereto? Newhaven-Dieppe, steerage passenger. Paris and back. Lapwing. Icarus." We are also given an insight into Stephen's sexual history in Dublin and Paris: "Am I a father? If I were?" The plot, as Eglinton comments, thickens.

'Wandering Rocks'

The narrative frame widens to take in the panorama of Dublin as characters criss-cross the city's streets. The events depicted are seemingly gratuitous, with nothing to unite them except that they appear in the novel. The 19 sections (or 18 and a coda) parallel the wandering rocks which Odysseus avoids having to encounter, and represent the disconnected and fragmented lives of Dublin's citizenry.

Just as the rocks never actually appear in the *Odyssey*, so nothing happens of any great note in this episode. The episode seems to wilfully navigate its way past any wider meaning, though the juxtaposition of the one-legged soldier who sings bitterly "– *For England ... home and beauty*" with the Viceregal Cavalcade that wends its way from the Viceregal Lodge in Phoenix Park through Dublin towards Ballsbridge suggests that Joyce is keen to locate the random and haphazard within the wider mechanisms of political and economic power and privilege. The inclusion of Father Conmee, the advertised speaker on Jesuit missions in the British colonies, only underscores this. There is also something of the Secret Police or the CCTV camera about the narrative: who is this omniscient narrator able to be in all places at once, and able to watch and listen in on the private actions of the characters. In this context, relatively innocent actions such as Miss Dunne "hid[ing] the Capel street library copy of the *Woman in White* far back in her drawer" assumes, and perhaps determines, a sense of universal guilt. Ironically, in creating such a narrator, Joyce can be seen as fulfilling the advice of William Parsons, third Earl of Rosse, who, in 1847, called for a police force in Ireland "especially devoted to the detection of crime" and with "an accurate knowledge of locality, and of the character and habits of almost every individual in the district".[6]

'Sirens'

Even in a novel of tours-des-forces, 'Sirens' is an astonishing achievement. Taking as its model, as Joyce described it, "all the eight regular parts of a *fuga per canonem*", the episode, to quote Walter Pater, "aspires towards the condition of music". Joyce being Joyce, however, is not content with pushing language as far as it can go in the direction of abstract musical sounds but he must offer a critique of Pater's artistic ideals. In doing so, of course, he mirrors Odysseus' desire to listen to the song of the Sirens while remaining unenchanted. He achieves this by requiring his men to tie him to the mast and to ignore his increasingly passionate entreaties that they release him. Joyce's masthead is Bloom, who listens to the various 'songs' that lull the other characters to their doom: alcoholism, Nationalism, sentimentality and women. That Joyce is himself half in love with the formal difficulties he set himself is only an additional temptation.

Interestingly, what saves him from writing what could easily have become a rather vapid literary exercise is his dedication to recording as accurately as possible the conversations, turns of phrase and sheer musicality of the ordinary Dubliner's way with language. Added to this, in Bloom's words, is Joyce's central argument with Pater's aesthetic: "Words? Music? No: it's what's behind." Even here, though, Bloom's thoughts partake of Kenner's theory of Joyce's "double writing": for while he is voicing his author's literary theory, he is also imaging the scene back in his and Molly's bedroom. It is now 4.00pm. – the hour of Blazes' assignation. Thus "the behind" in question is also Molly's as Boylan, "pulsing proud erect", enters her. Not for Molly, then, the missionary position.

Other betrayals have their part in the episode, most notably in the narrative of 'The Croppy Boy', references to which have cropped up already in the novel, and which Ben Dollard now sings to the hushed customers of the Ormond Hotel bar. The words of the song punctuate Bloom's interior monologue, telling of the betrayal and subsequent murder of the eponymous croppy boy, who confesses his support for a free Ireland to what he thinks is a priest ("At the siege of Ross did my father fall,/And at Gorey my loving brothers all,/I alone am left of my name and race,/I will go to Wexford and take their place./.../ I bear no hate against living thing/But I love my country above the King.") only to find that he has betrayed himself to a British soldier in disguise. An anthem of the Home Rule movement, the song assumes a further ironic meaning in the context of Bloom's domestic situation.

'Cyclops'

Though Bloom leaves the Ormond Hotel before Dollard finishes his song (Bloom is unsympathetic to the "voice of penance and of grief" which "holds [the listeners] like birdlime"), he is unable to escape so easily the Siren call of Nationalism.

The Citizen, or to give him his Homeric name, Polyphemus, is the epitome of the one-eyed bigot. In our own time, he is the *Daily Mail* incarnate: 'many-voiced' he may be, but as the episode progresses his mood swings from the cantankerous to the xenophobic and homicidal. The Homeric parallels are further instructive in that Polyphemus is the son of Poseidon, who appears in the novel as

Britannia with her trident holding sway over the oceans of the world. Irish Nationalism, Joyce is saying, is the direct result of Imperial rule, and it was for this reason that he rejected the narrowness of those like the Citizen and his nameless sidekick (the narrator of the episode) who see everything in terms of simple binary oppositions. To do so, *Ulysses* warns, is simply to play the coloniser on their own terms. "Both," as Seamus Deane says, "shared the same premises, each legitimizing itself in terms of a national, providentially ratified 'story' or 'history'". Other means of resistance are called for, more imaginative, more playful and therefore more subversive.

The literary form the episode adopts is that of hyperbole, though the irony is that the narrator would not recognise his narrative style as such. Bloom's encounter with the Citizen and his increasingly drunken cronies is narrated in a wide range of parodic styles, hence the essential 'many-voicedness' of the episode. Parody, however, becomes a form of extremism. This many-voicedness leads to textual instability, or untrustworthiness; parody to exaggeration and ultimately a loss of perspective (exactly what we would expect from the one-eyed Cyclops). Thus the cigar Bloom accepts from the Citizen rather than join him in a drink is first described as a "prime stinker", before becoming a "knockmedown cigar" and finally a "tuppeny stump". What is at stake here isn't the metaphorical quality of Stephen's hat, for example; rather the change in nomenclature is swayed by the Citizen's and the narrator's increasingly vociferous hatred of Bloom because he is a Jew:

> – What is your nation if I may ask, says the citizen.
> – Ireland, says Bloom. I was born here. Ireland.
> The citizen said nothing only cleared the spit out of his gullet and, gob, he spat a Red bank oyster out of him right in the corner. [p. 272]

The position Bloom is being forced to occupy is akin to the situation that has faced countless émigrés and refugees throughout history, the consequences of which have been written about by Amin Maalouf:

> We cannot be satisfied with forcing billions of bewildered human beings to choose between excessive assertion of their identity and the loss of their identity and the loss of their

identity altogether, between fundamentalism and disintegration. [I]f they feel they have to choose between denial of the self and denial of the other – then we shall be bringing into being legions of the lost and hordes of bloodthirsty madmen.

Maalouf is writing about the current crisis facing relations between the Western and Islamic worlds. What he is saying here, however, is pertinent to turn-of-the-twentieth century relations between Ireland and Britain, relations that resulted in the partition of Ireland and a century of still unresolved conflict.

By the end of the episode Bloom is personally to blame for all Ireland's troubles, and in their drunkenness the men round on him: "It'd be an act of God to take a hold of a fellow the like of that and throw him in the bloody sea. Justifiable homicide, so it would." It hardly needs stating that what is being advocated is ethnic cleansing: "– Saint Patrick would want to land again … and convert us, says the Citizen, after allowing things like that to contaminate our shores." Bloom's response is emphatic and profoundly moving:

> – But it's no use, says he. Force, hatred, history, all that. That's not life for men and women, insult and hatred. And everybody knows that it's the very opposite of that that is really life.
> – What? Says Alf.
> – Love, says Bloom. I mean the opposite of hatred. [p. 273]

'Nausicaa'

With its onanistic fantasies or, as Joyce described it, "specially new frigging style", 'Nausicaa' was the straw that broke the back of the New York Society for the Suppression of Vice. The editors of the *Little Review*, where *Ulysses* was being serialised, were convicted of publishing obscenity and publication of the novel ceased. This was in 1920/21. Not until December 1933 and the ruling of Federal Judge John M. Woolsey was the ban on the novel lifted in the United States. It is perhaps useful in the context of this episode to quote in full a paragraph of Woolsey's judgement:

> I am quite aware that owing to some of its scenes *Ulysses* is a rather strong draught to ask some sensitive, though normal, persons to take. But my considered opinion, after long reflection, is that whilst in many places the effect of *Ulysses*

on the reader undoubtedly is somewhat emetic, nowhere does it tend to be an aphrodisiac. *Ulysses* may, therefore, be admitted into the United States.

In the leap from one kind of literary technique to another the reader can sometimes lose sight of the close connections between episodes. This has led to the charge that the novel is lacking in organic unity. 'Wandering Rocks' and 'Sirens', however, are linked by the sound of the Viceregal's horses going past the Ormond Hotel. In turn, 'Cyclops' and 'Nausicaa' are connected by the fact that Gerty McDowell, the subject of Bloom's "emetic" voyeurism, is the Citizen's granddaughter. Though not immediately recognisable, other parallels exist. For just as the Citizen is a parody of Irish Nationalism, so Gerty is a parody of Irish womanhood with Joyce deliberately parodying Stephen's epiphany on the beach in *A Portrait*. And just as 'Cyclops' is governed by the discourse of Nationalism, so Gerty is determined by, among many others, the conventions of romantic fiction, fashion magazines, advertising, cliché and Mariolatry (the worship of the Virgin Mary). We might go further and see Bloom's responses as being equally limited and limiting:

> Mr Bloom watched her as she limped away. Poor girl! That's why she's left on the shelf ... Jilted beauty. A defect is ten times worse in a woman. But makes them polite. Glad I didn't know it when she was on show. Hot little devil all the same. I wouldn't mind. Curiosity like a nun or a negress or a girl with glasses ... Near her monthlies, I expect, makes them feel ticklish ... Virgins go mad in the end I suppose. [p. 301]

And so his thoughts continue. What is shocking about the episode, then, isn't that Bloom masturbates while an adolescent girl allows him to peek up her skirts; rather that the form both their fantasy worlds take is a closed circuit of hearsay, prejudice and cliché. Even here Bloom betrays masculine sexual behaviour as being a militarised zone: "Every bullet has its billet."

'Oxen of the Sun'

Joyce takes those elements of parody and ventriloquism that mark the two previous episodes and here uses them to provide a summary of the growth of English, and in some cases Anglo-Irish literature. This growth is meant to parallel that of the foetus in the womb, the episode being set at 10.00pm in the Holles Street Maternity Hospital where Stephen and a gaggle of medical students are awaiting the arrival of Buck Mulligan while Mrs Purefoy struggles upstairs to give birth to a son. The men are drunk and their bawdy talk shows little respect for either their surroundings or for women. What also links the episode to those previous is the series of transformations Bloom undergoes. Among other guises he is referred to as a "wayfarer" (Anglo-Saxon), the "traveller Leopold" (Mandeville), "childe Leopold" (Malory), "Mr Cautious Calmer" (Bunyan) and "the johnny in the black duds" (slang).

Joyce himself described 'Oxen of the Sun' as "the most difficult episode ... to interpret and execute", and it is unlikely that there will be many readers who will disagree. From the thrice-repeated opening sentence – "Deshil Holles Eamus" – which is intended to mimic the formalised chants of Roman fertility rites through to the eruption of a veritable Pentecost of vernaculars, the reader clings to the familiar like a shipwrecked sailor to a piece of driftwood.

The episode also marks the coming together of the different paths which Stephen and Bloom have traversed during the day. Bloom's fears for Mrs Purefoy and his memories of his own dead son fuse in his growing tenderness and fatherly affection for Stephen who, deep in his cups, is obsessed by aspects of Catholic theology and his own aesthetics. At one point he gives a brief sermon, the burden of which is that the Word is made flesh in a woman's womb, but our flesh (or biographical experiences) are transformed through the intercession of the Holy Spirit (or artist) into the Word.

The episode ends with the safe delivery of Mortimer Edward Purefoy and Stephen and Lynch, having parted from the rest of their company outside Burke's pub, are shepherded by the sober and watchful Bloom as they enter the precincts of Nighttown and its brothels.

'Circe'

If 'Oxen of the Sun' signals the dark night of the soul so far as the reader and comprehensibility are concerned, 'Circe' plunges Stephen and Bloom into a nightmarish world where they find it difficult to differentiate between the very real dangers of Dublin's red light district and the no less perilous inner world of their unconscious fears and desires. Nighttown is both a geographical location and a state of mind. It is a place where thoughts become actions, and so the episode is written in the style of a drama. Like a number of Byron's plays, however, it is not written to be performed. It is a drama for, and of, the mind. Having said this, there are affinities between Joyce's 'staging' of the unconscious and Artaud's Theatre of Cruelty or the theatrical experiments of the Dadaists and the German Expressionists. We should also not ignore the fact that for all the surreal imagery of the episode what is notable throughout are the ways in which Bloom and Stephen's thoughts are determined by external forms of governance. As in 'Nausicaa', ideology determines fantasy and imagination. In short, the episode is a vivid reminder that discourse roots itself not only in external actions but in our deepest selves.

If Bloom's fantasies revolve around his frustrated sex life he is also clearly anxious about nationality and belonging, as he is about his passivity of character:

> My old dad was a J.P. I'm as staunch a Britisher as you are, sir. I fought with the colours for king and country in the absentminded war under general Gough in the park and was disabled at Spion Kop and Bloemfontein [.] [p. 800]

What is doubly notable in this speech, however, is that Bloom has internalised the wider sense of guilt and shame surrounding the Boer War. For "absentminded" we might read 'denial'. References to the South Africa campaign are scattered throughout *Ulysses*, never more so than in this episode where military, economic and sexual life are shown as co-dependent: Bella Cohen's son, we discover, is a student at Oxford where his education will be paid for from by money his mother makes prostituting young women to the colonised and colonisers alike; and Private Carr and Private Compton, two serving British soldiers, appear as redcoats, their "tunics bloodbright in a lampglow". What the episode does, then, is to point up, in Sandra F. Siegel's phrase, "the discrepancy between the ideology [Britain] professes and the ideology [Britain] practises".

When Stephen and Bloom are turned out of Bella Cohen's brothel, it is the soldiers (with a cameo role from Tennyson quoting his own

'Charge of the Light Brigade', a poem that memorialises British losses in the Crimean War) who threaten to reassert the status quo:

PRIVATE COMPTON

He doesn't half want a thick ear, the blighter. Biff him one, Harry.

PRIVATE CARR

(*to Cissy*) Was he insulting you while me and him was having a piss?

LORD TENNYSON

(*gentleman poet in Union Jack blazer and cricket flannels, bareheaded, flowingbearded*) Theirs not to reason why.

PRIVATE COMPTON

Biff him, Harry. [p. 480]

Stephen tries to engage Carr in dialogue, but the terms of his engagement only rile the soldiers more:

You die for your country. Suppose. (*he places his arm on Private Carr's sleeve*) Not that I wish it for you. But I say: Let my country die for me. Up to the present it has done so. I didn't want it to die. Damn death. Long live life! [p. 482]

Joyce clearly modelled Stephen and Carr's set-to on William Blake's near-fatal involvement with a certain Private Scofield in 1803 when Blake, having forcibly removed Scofield from the garden of his cottage in Felpham, was subsequently charged with sedition, a capital offence in an England living in fear of Napoleonic invasion. The parallels with Blake are underscored by Stephen's drunkenly misquoting one of Blake's 'Auguries of Innocence', thus rewriting Blake's original and establishing a provocative counter-reading of the extent to which the misery and economic disenfranchisement of the British Empire reach: "The harlot's cry from street to street/Shall weave Old Ireland's windingsheet."

Stephen is now beset by a host of figures from either side of the Irish sea, each representing a facet of Empire and Nationalism: Edward the Seventh, Kevin Egan (the Fenian with a penchant for "gunpowder cigarettes" whom Stephen has met in Paris), a host of Catholic priests offering up a Black Mass (with Stephen as the sacrificial lamb), The Citizen and, with a noose around his neck, the Croppy Boy. Again, Bloom uses the Boer War to attempt to distract the soldiers and to test the irony of Irish loyalty: "We fought for you in South Africa, Irish missile troops. Isn't that history?" It is hard not to see events as marking the apotheosis of Stephen who assumes a kind of Christ-like dignity in being knocked cold by Carr. The first thing on his mind when he comes to is Yeats' poem 'Who Goes with Fergus', returning us to the opening episode where Stephen remembers singing the same song to his mother on her deathbed. The episode culminates in Bloom's vision of his dead son Rudy carrying, Christ-like, a baby lamb.

'Eumaeus'

With the help of Corny Kelleher, Bloom and Stephen escape Nighttown and the two Constables who arrive too late to avoid Stephen's assault but are nevertheless intent on being "unscrupulous in the service of the Crown". In 'Eumaeus', then, we find Stephen and Bloom taking refuge in a cabmen's shelter. It is now 1.00am. The novel has entered its final stage. The *Nostos* has begun.

In terms of the *Odyssey* the episode parallels Odysseus' arrival home to Ithaca and the necessity of his remaining disguised. Thus Bloom refuses to divulge his identity to the inquiries of the other men in the shelter, though Stephen is more forthcoming. As it is, the "redbearded sailor" who asks the question and says that he knows Stephen's father, mistakes him for a different Dedalus: "He [Simon Dedalus] toured the wide world with Hengler's Royal Circus." Such mistaken or undisclosed identities dominate the episode, leading us to imagine that there exist parallel worlds in which characters sharing the same names as these wander round the streets of an identical-but-different Dublin. The episode is a series of false starts and tautologies, as though meaning itself were trying to cover its tracks. As such we must remain vigilant. As Jeri Johnson notes:

> Omniscient (authorial) narrator, Stephen, Bloom dissolve and merge in an indirect discourse so free as to be virtually unattributable. And, while the language of the characters is

absorbed by the narrative, everything is infected with a tendency to an exhausted, verbose, constantly misfiring, sententious, logorrhoeic, never-use-one-word-when-thirty-will-do kind of prolixity.

Everyone in the episode appears under what we assume is an alias. Bloom, whose original name is Virag and who also trades under the name Henry Flower, now appears in the published list of mourners present at Dignam's funeral as "L. Boom". Little wonder that he is "all at sea" and unable to "make head or tail of the whole business". Also all at sea, Skin-the-Goat prophesises, is the British Empire:

> [A] day of reckoning, he stated *crescendo* with no uncertain voice, thoroughly monopolising all the conversation, was in store for mighty England, despite her power of pelf on account of her crimes. ... The Boers were the beginning of the end. Brummagem England was toppling already and her downfall would be Ireland, her Achilles heel[.] [p. 523]

Throughout there are echoes of the opening pages of *A Portrait* where Joyce makes it impossible to distinguish between Stephen and his father. Here, however, the blurring of identities is between father and adopted son. In doing so the way is prepared for the following episode where Bloom becomes "Bloom Stoom" and Stephen "Stephen Blephen". Stephen, however, sees in such textual uncertainty not confusion but liberation: "We can't change the country. Let us change the subject."

'Ithaca'

It is 2.00am and Bloom has taken Stephen home to Eccles Street. Molly is upstairs in bed. For the first time in the novel, then, Odysseus, Telemachus and Penelope are together under the same roof. The irony, of course, is that the Bloom household is far from its mythic ideal. As in *A Portrait* where the calamitous Christmas dinner scene plays out in miniature the wider discord of Irish society following the death of Parnell, so at the end of 'Eumaeus' it is possible to see that 7 Eccles Street becomes the stage on which the same themes of passion and betrayal are acted out. What complicates this scenario is that Bloom, who in 'Circe' is hailed by John Howard Parnell as "Illustrious

Bloom! Successor to my famous brother", is the cuckolded husband and it is Boylan who can be seen as acting the part of Parnell. Such mistaken or misattributed identities are all part of the alienated narratives of 'Eumaeus'. In 'Ithaca', however, we surely have a right to expect these matters to be clarified.

That Joyce called the episode "a mathematical catechism" in which "events are resolved into their cosmic physical, psychical, etc equivalents" certainly seems to suggest that such will be the case. As a result we seem to have left narrative fiction behind and entered the realm of cold facts, with the episode serving as an encyclopaedia to the novel as a whole. Thus we learn things about the characters that we haven't so far been told. The episode is about the 'whatness', the 'whereness' and the 'whyness' of the world. In this it might remind us of a child constantly asking questions, seeking reassurance, testing the limits of its parents' knowledge and patience. Yet for all the impersonality of the writing the episode is poetic, emphasising that poetry is in itself a way of knowing and being present in the world. To take a single example:

> What spectacle confronted them when they, first the host, then the guest, emerged silently, doubly dark, from obscurity by a passage from the rere of the house into the penumbra of the garden?
>
> The heaventree of stars hung with humid nightblue fruit. [p. 573]

The stars and the constellations make frequent appearances in 'Ithaca', drawing our attention to the fact that, as François Hartog has said in relation to the Homeric world, "human beings mark out their territory, always ephemeral, ever needing to be reconquered, in between the gods and the beasts."[7] What Bloom needs to reconquer, of course, is his own home and, after the bestial transformations of 'Circe' and the anonymity of 'Eumaeus', his identity and humanity. Whether he does so is left ambiguous. Throughout the day Bloom has had rattling round his mind the advertising slogan for Plumtree's Potted Meat: "What is home without/Plumtree's Potted Meat?/ Incomplete./With it an abode of bliss." Climbing into bed, however, he discovers the remains of Molly and Boylan's love-feast:

What did his limbs, when gradually extended, encounter?

> New clean bedlinen, additional odours, the presence of human
> form, female, hers, the imprint of a human form, male, not
> his, some crumbs, some flakes of potted meat, recooked, which
> he removed. [p. 601]

Perhaps at no point else in the novel is the gulf between Homer's *Odyssey* and *Ulysses* so painfully wide.

At the close of the episode Bloom falls asleep. His doing so is likened to a child in the womb. This is not the only origin to which Bloom returns:

> Where?
> •   [p. 607]

Thus *Ulysses* takes leave of Bloom. At the end he returns to being simply a dot of ink on the page.

'Penelope'

In the *Odyssey* Penelope keeps her suitors at arm's length by promising to make a decision about which one she will marry only after she has finished weaving a tapestry. Every night, however, she sits up and unravels the day's additions. Thus she hopes to forestall the day when she has to choose between the memory of a husband who may be long dead and the suitors who want to take control of her and the island.

Molly, too, works hard at unpicking everything her author has achieved, remaking it in her own image. Indeed at one point we catch her addressing Joyce directly: "O Jamesy let me up out of this pooh sweets of sin". Elsewhere she threatens to wrest control of the novel away from Joyce and write her own version of events: "I declare somebody ought to put him in the budget if I only could remember the 1 half of the thing and write a book out of it the works of Master Poldy". In this Joyce is bringing the novel full circle, reminding us that it is Haines' intention to edit a book of Stephen's sayings. But while in 'Telemachus' we recognise an Englishman wanting to take textual control of the Irishman, in Molly we see Joyce's attempts at female emancipation. If 'Nausicaa' exposed the discourses that construct Femininity and 'Oxen of the Sun' the institutionalised control men have over reproduction and childbirth, 'Penelope' remains a radical attempt at allowing a female consciousness to speak free of censure. In part we can see this as Joyce resurrecting the mother he always feared that he had killed. He admitted such fears to Nora, who reproached him by calling him a "Woman-killer". Nora was equally forthright about *Ulysses*, which she thought 'swinish' (*"das Buch ist ein Schwein"*) and Joyce's limited understanding of the female: "He knows nothing at all about women." This is as true of Joyce as it is of Bloom, of course. What marks Bloom out from the other men in the novel is, as even Molly accedes, his ability to make the effort to understand and to empathise: "that was why I liked him because I saw he understood or felt what a woman is".

If Molly's soliloquy is a rewriting of everything that has gone before in the novel (as, indeed, is each episode), it also reinforces those aspects of the novel which I have been concentrating on here. Molly was born on Gibraltar, taken from the Spanish by Britain in 1704. Her father was a major in the British army, and she is proud of the standing this gives her among other women: "soldiers daughter am I ay ... theyd die down dead off their feet if ever they got a chance of walking down the Alameda on an officers arm like me". Apolitical, she condemns the Boer war not out of hatred for Empire but for more personal reasons: "that clumsy Claddagh ring for luck that I gave Gardner going to south Africa where those Boers killed him with their war and fever". In one of the many inversions of the Homeric parallels, therefore, it isn't Bloom/Ulysses who murders Molly/Penelope's suitors but Poseidon/Britannia. Molly is equally suspicious of the promises of domestic politics, referring to Bloom's convictions as though they were so many pieces of paste jewellery: "and all the Doyles said he was going to stand for a member of Parliament O wasn't I the born fool to believe all his blather about home rule". Apart of, and yet apart from, British military rule, her speech is distinguished by the number of Spanish and Gaelic words and phrases that she uses. Whether we are to read this as signalling that Molly is one of the appropriators or one of the appropriated remains ambiguous. What we can say for sure is that Joyce allows her the last word – "Yes" – the first and last letters of which, as it were, "brings us by a commodius vicus of recirculation" back to the novel's first utterance: "Stately, plump Buck Mulligan".

In a sense, then, there is no homecoming in *Ulysses*. Or rather, every homecoming simply prepares us for the act of re-reading this most inexhaustible of books. What her "Yes" also signifies is Molly's triumph over the myth of Penelope. At the last she has unwoven the construct of the faithful, hearth-bound wife and has asserted her own physical and mental presence in the novel. She insists on modernity. In doing so, of course, she signals the disparity that has existed from the beginning between *Ulysses* and its Hellenic forerunner. This is a far cry from Kenner's conclusion that Molly claims authority over "this animal kingdom of the dead" which, it seems to me, plays into the hands of those who would dismiss 'Penelope' as a product of Joyce's misogyny. No, in allowing the last word to belong to Molly, Joyce moves, as Fredric Jameson points out, "well beyond that moment of classical modernism and its ideologies ... in which the very notion of some mythic unity and reconciliation was used in a ... fetishised way."[8] Homer's *Odyssey* as a point of origin or of arrival – in short, of deferral – is whipped away from under us like a magician removing the tablecloth while leaving the crockery still standing.

Footnotes

[1] 'Ulysses', *The Cambridge Companion to James Joyce*, pp. 131-159.

[2] Joyce's decision to declare his political beliefs in newspaper articles written for a non-Irish audience parallels the lectures Oscar Wilde gave on 19th-century Irish poets during his visit to North America in 1882. More usually thought of as the archetypal a-political dandy, Wilde's lectures declared him to be a nationalist: "When Ireland gains her independence, its schools of art and other educational branches will be revived and Ireland will regain the proud position she once held among the nations of Europe". See 'Oscar Wilde's Gift and Oxford's "Coarse Impertince"', Sandra F. Siegel in *Ideology and Ireland in the Nineteenth Century*, pp. 69-78.

[3] *On Identity* (1998), translated Barbara Bray (The Harvill Press: London, 2000).

[4] From 'The Nightmare of History' (1961), *Modern Critical Views: James Joyce*, pp. 21-37.

[5] John Berger, *And Our Faces, My Heart, Brief as Photos* (Vintage

International: New York, 1991).

⁶ See 'Maria Edgeworth and the Aesthetics of Secrecy' by Willa Murphy.
⁷ *Memories of Odysseus: Frontier Tales From Ancient Greece* (1996), trans. Janet Lloyd (Edinburgh University Press: Edinburgh, 2001).
⁸ '*Ulysses* in History' (1982), *Modern Critical Views: James Joyce*, pp. 173-188.

5

Slip and Slop: *Finnegans Wake*

"Belief in trauma as a kind of agency, as a cultural force – in events as the real heroes and heroines in life stories," Adam Phillips has written, " – turns up historically when people are beginning to lose faith in God and character and cause and effect. [T]he idea of trauma reassures us that we can find a beginning, and that there is a beginning worth finding. It puts a plot, if not a plan, back into modern lives."[1] Phillips goes on to ascribe this belief in trauma – or original sin – as a key aspect of Modernism, particularly among those writers who thought western culture had got rid of "the assured place of the artist".

As Karen Lawrence has argued, Joyce's strategy in *Finnegans Wake* is to attack the idea that art is in any way a simple process of self-expression or autobiography, or that the writer should be assured some privileged position of authority over the text they have written. While this is hardly new in Joyce's oeuvre – we need only think of Molly's unravelling of *Ulysses,* for example – what is are the lengths to which he went in inscribing this process in the very structure and language of this, his last work. In Lawrence's words the novel becomes "a complicated embedding, disguising, dispersing of the author and his desire in the text."[2] For Joyce, then, the disintegration of hierarchical certainties meant the overthrow of various other forms of authority: imperial, economic and patriarchal. Seeing these things as implicated in himself, and him in them, Joyce therefore needed to find a means of unsettling the hitherto privileged status of the author. Similarly Joyce disrupted and then remoulded our expectations of language and its structures, almost as though he had anticipated Wittgenstein's asking that we "Think of words as instruments characterised by their use, and then think of the use of a hammer, the use of a chisel, the use of a square, of a pot of glue"[3] and that he began, Picasso-like, to improvise with whatever materials lay to hand and to proceed by association.

Finnegans Wake, we should remind ourselves, was written during the two decades that followed the cataclysm of the First World War and the radical restructuring of Europe's internal borders that came about after the treaties of Versailles (1919) and Trianon (1920). The Austro-Hungarian Empire was dismantled, and Britain's ability to assert control over its vast empire was showing signs of strain. Joyce had experienced some of these things firsthand. Returning to Trieste in 1919 he found the place greatly changed as a result of the war and by the terms of the Treaty of Saint-Germain by which the city, in which the Italian language and culture had long flourished, was removed from Austrian control and assigned to Italy. Ireland, too, as we will see, was not exempt from change. Further afield, America was beginning to flex its economic muscle, and the Bolshevik-led revolution in Russia meant that communism was being implemented on a scale that would have left Marx and Engels breathless. Women were increasingly given access to the democratic process through the power to vote, as were the working classes. The world depicted in *Ulysses* was suddenly beginning to look very old-fashioned. This is immediately clear when we consider that in *Ulysses* the printed word still dominates the dissemination of information, while *Finnegans Wake* gives us a world in which exist radio, television and cinema.

The implosion of those cultural 'certainties' that existed pre-1914 was for Joyce and others a release of enormous creative energy. As we have seen, he rejected the binary structures that underpin Western culture because every such structure – male/female, black/white – is premised on the (often implicit) assumption that one of the pair maintains an advantage over the other. It might be helpful, then, to think of *Finnegans Wake* as a full-frontal assault on the binaries of author/reader. Joyce, then, accepted the new world of contingency, accident, mess and disorder – words, as Adam Phillips points out, that more often than not are descriptive of the feminine – and relocated desire not in power but in abjection. Or, as Bloom puts it: "Dirty cleans."

While such an analysis may seem to play into the hands of critics such as Sandra Gilbert and Susan Gubar who "refused to be

Mollified" by "feminologist reJoyceings"[4], it can be argued that *Finnegans Wake* is far from being Joyce's attempt at papering over or synthesising the very real differences and antagonisms that exist between men and women in society, and between the Masculine and Feminine aspects of our psyche, but rather a coming clean that such tensions pertain at every level of our social and psychological selves. Out of necessity, then, the novel is a 'his-story' of repression, arguably the most telling representative of which is Shem the Penman, a comic self-portrait of the artist as an ageing man, who makes ink out of his own bodily waste and uses his skin as paper:

> when the call comes, he shall produce nichthemerically from his unheavenly body a no uncertain quantity of obscene matter not protected by copriright in the United States of Ourania ... with this double dye, brought to blood heat, gallic acid on iron ore, through the bowels of his misery, flashly, faithly, nastily [written] over every square inch of the only foolscap available, his own body[.] [p. 185]

In Shem we might say that Joyce was anticipating the concerns of contemporary artists such as Marc Quinn – whose *Self* (1991) is made from eight pints of Quinn's own blood kept frozen in the form of a bust of the artist – Tracey Emin – whose infamous *My Bed* (1998/9) was constructed from the actual debris of her life and included soiled sheets, vodka bottles, underwear, condoms and polaroids – or Chris Ofili – who has used elephant dung to decorate the surface of some of his paintings. Just as these artists break taboos regarding the relationship between the artist's body and the corpus of their art, biography and biology, textual certainty and the messiness of our emotional lives, so Joyce makes demands on our ability to accept that such materials and subject matter are appropriate to high art. What the novel insistently demands of us is that we take it on its own unique terms. In doing so it provokes a very real problem: how readable is *Finnegans Wake*?

This question will almost certainly have arisen for everyone who has set out to read all of Joyce's books. Many will not have had to wait to reach *Finnegans Wake* before such doubts appear. For some it might be the long sermon on hell in *A Portrait*; for others it will be 'Proteus' or 'Oxen of the Sun'. All, I would hazard a guess, will very soon ask it of *Finnegans Wake*, probably as early as the third paragraph and the hundred-letter word that is the sound of thunder accompanying the Fall. Even advocates of the novel admit its difficulties. Seamus Deane, for example, pulls no punches in his Introduction: "The first thing to say about *Finnegans Wake* is that it is, in an important sense, unreadable." Margot Norris, too, acknowledges the difficulties of the novel, but sees them as inherent in the subject matter: "The indeterminacy of *Finnegans Wake* is created by the strange ontological conditions the work explores, particularly dreaming and dying, conditions that call the being of the self, and self-identity, into radical question."[5] John Gross, much less of an admirer, speaks for many when he says that "An elementary problem looms up at the outset: we are dealing with a book which is largely incomprehensible at a first reading, and not much clearer at a second".

Whatever our doubts about the novel, Joyce seems to have got there first:

> it is not a nice production. It is a pinch of scribble, not wortha bottle of cabbis! Overdrawn! Puffedly offal tosh! Besides its auctionable, all about crime and libel! Nothing beyond clerical horrors *et omnibus* to be entered for the foreign as secondclass matter. The fuellest filth ever fired ... Flummery is what I would call it if you were to ask me to put it on a single dimension what pronounced opinion I might possibly orally have about them bagses of trash which the mother and Mr Unmentionable (O breed not his same!) has reduced to writing[.] [pp. 419-20]

Along with difficulty and obscurity comes boredom. What we mean by boredom in terms of a novel, of course, will be different for each reader. We might, though, agree that any novel that loses track of the plot over an extended period of time would try our patience, as will a novel the narrator and narrative style/s of which are constantly changing. If we agree that this is an accurate description of *Finnegans Wake* – what the novel itself calls "the continually more and less intermisunderstanding minds of the anticollaborators" – we will also have to agree that to greater and lesser extents it also describes *A Portrait* and *Ulysses*. What then is different about *Finnegans Wake*?

To begin to answer this it may be useful to return briefly to the conditions of its creation. For while readers frustrated by the novel might wish it different, there can be little doubt that Joyce must have felt something similar. In his case, however, he must have wished the messiness of the world and his personal circumstances other than they were.

Joyce found his new work difficult to get started. It seems that he made some notes for the book in October 1922, but wasn't able to develop them until March the following year. By the autumn of 1923 he had completed half-a-dozen sketches. Having found a sense of direction he worked steadily over the next two years or so to complete what we now have as Parts I and III. It was at this point that he met Eugene and Maria Jolas, ex-pat Americans living in Paris. Eugene Jolas was fluent in several languages, and was searching for a theory of art which, in Ellmann's description:

> would also be a philosophy of life ... a 'religion of the word', the ritual of which [Jolas] saturated with terms like 'phantastic', 'mantic', and his neologism, 'paramyth.' Art alone could be trusted, and trusted only if it abjured externality in the name of imagination.

Jolas and his wife quickly set about founding a review they called *transition*. Subtitling it 'An International Quarterly for Creative Experiment' they offered to publish Joyce's *Work in Progress*, the working title for his, as yet, unfinished book. As with *A Portrait* and *Ulysses*, guaranteed publication led Joyce to hurriedly begin revising what he had written. As a result, the first chapter was published in *transition* in 1927, though some initial fragments had been published three years earlier in *transatlantic review*. Subsequently Joyce found work on the novel heavy-going, largely for personal reasons. Between 1923 and 1930 he underwent ten painful eye operations; his father died in December 1931; and from 1932 his daughter, Lucia, became increasingly ill with what was diagnosed as schizophrenia. Clearly, then, there are aspects of *Finnegans Wake* that reflect tensions in Joyce himself: the death of an often violent and overbearing father whom Joyce nevertheless adored; and the eruption of disorder in the illness of his daughter. Other tensions arose when those individuals who had previously supported and encouraged Joyce in his writing began to be openly critical of the direction his new book was taking. Not least among those who turned on *Work in Progress* was Joyce's brother, Stanislaus: "It is unspeakably wearisome ... the witless wandering of literature before its final extinction ... I for one would not read more than a paragraph of it, if I did not know you." Similarly there were events in the wider world that caused Joyce anxiety. Between 1916 and 1922 Ireland had been transformed from a colony and a constitutional part of the United Kingdom to a country partitioned into two states, the Irish Free State and the province of Northern Ireland. As is invariably the case, partition of the country resulted in a brief but nasty civil war which Nora and her two children experienced first-hand in 1922 when, visiting Galway, the train in which they were travelling was caught in crossfire.

The underlying connection between this turn of events and the composition and themes of *Finnegans Wake*, particularly the ways in which it interrogates the idea of the Fall and the origin of original sin (or 'trauma', in Phillips' terms), shouldn't be underestimated. As Seamus Deane comments: "For fifty years before the publication of the *Wake*, [Ireland] had been engaged in rewriting its past in the hope of realizing for itself a future other than that of a peculiar kind of colony". Following the Civil war of 1922-23, however, the country turned in on itself, declaring that, Deane continues, "it had remained traditional, anti-modern, loyal to the old [Catholic] faith and to the pieties that the old faith claimed were integral to the Irish heritage and its own teaching." Joyce's long-held fears of Ireland and Irishness becoming 'essentialised' in terms of tradition, heritage, destiny – those "big words," Stephen tells Mr Deasy, "which make us so unhappy" – must have seemed to have been realised. As R.F. Foster has commented, "an intrinsic component of the [Easter Uprising] (for all the pluralist window-dressing of the Proclamation issued by Pearse*) was the strain of mystic Catholicism identifying the Irish soul as Catholic and Gaelic." Indeed, the language of Christian blood-

---

* Patrick William Pearse (1879-1916) was a prominent member of the Gaelic League, and following the Easter Uprising became head of the Provisional Government of the Irish Republic. He was captured by the British Army and executed alongside 14 other leaders of the Uprising in May 1916.

sacrifice was explicitly used to justify and explain the events of Easter 1916. "Life springs from death," declared Pearse, "and from the graves of patriotic men and women spring living nations."

Wider events soon caught up with the writing and publication of the book, and the personal lives of Joyce and his family. In September 1939, Britain and France declared war on Germany. Life in Paris was made unbearable by the constant fear of aerial bombardment, a fear that Lucia found particularly difficult to manage. "We're going downhill fast," Joyce told Samuel Beckett. Whether he meant his family alone or the world at large isn't clear.

Unlike the narratives of his earlier works, *Finnegans Wake* avoids easy summary. So much so that specialist opinion is often divided on what exactly is 'happening' or who is talking (and about what) at certain points. For a critic such as Stephen Heath, this is implicit in all of Joyce's works, and he warns against the tendency to read Joyce in terms of continuity of identity. The particular challenge of *Finnegans Wake*, in Heath's words, is that it is "a hesitation of meaning into the perpetual 'later'". This is useful in as much as it returns us to ideas discussed earlier: Benjamin's notion of the "afterlife" of works, and Stephen's insistence on the importance of the present perpetually giving way to the future.

Though there is a 'story', that of the Fall, it is a story that is repeated over and over again from different perspectives. Associated with it are two abiding questions: What was it, and what were, or are, its consequences? As we might expect there is also a preoccupation with sex and guilt. As in earlier works, Joyce locates these themes in the life of a family – the Earwicker family of Chapelizod, a Dublin suburb – consisting of Humphrey Chimpden Earwicker (HCE), the Rabelesian father and pub landlord; his wife, Anna Livia Plurabelle (ALP); their twin sons, Shem and Shaun; and a daughter called variously Isabel, Issy, Iseult or Isolde and who has a split personality. We will get some sense of the complexity of these 'characters' when we add that contained in HCE (Here Comes Everybody) are all men of enterprise throughout history and from every kind of story; that ALP is every homekeeper; the twins every pair of brothers or opponents; and Issy every beautiful woman. In addition to these roles, HCE is also a primordial giant and a mountain, and his wife a river, a principle of nature who, in Seamus Heaney's words, "comes babbling and bubbling up out of the fluvial, pluvial, hithering, thithering waters of the Dublin night".

In many ways the book picks up where *Ulysses* left off. Just as the last word of *Ulysses* ineluctably returns us to the first, so the first and last sentences of *Finnegans Wake* are in fact halves of the same sentence held apart for over 600 pages. There are other similarities. For example, the last page of *Ulysses* has Molly remembering how she gave Bloom "the bit of seedcake out of [her] mouth", an image clearly associated with the Garden of Eden and Eve giving Adam the fruit of the Tree of Knowledge to eat. Similarly, the theme of sexual betrayal and voyeurism that runs throughout *Ulysses* is paralleled in *Finnegans Wake* by the family's awareness that HCE has performed some sort of crime, sexual in nature, with a young girl (or girls) who may be his daughter in the Phoenix Park, Dublin's own Garden of Eden, and which two soldiers (and possibly Shem) witnessed. It is the characters' inability to talk openly about these things (hence the confusion about exactly what has happened) that results in the fact that the novel is set at night and told through dreams. To otherwise speak of the crime is taboo. The form of the novel, then, reflects the repression of this crime and how it bubbles up through language and the characters' consciousness. Associated with this repression is the establishment of patriarchy: how the male represses and legislates the incestuous desire he has for the female. Countering this masculine aspect of the novel is the voice of ALP, the mother who will redeem language and her writer son, Shem, from the authority of the Father.

Clearly, then, the single referential myth that sustains the complex narrative of *Ulysses*, however iconoclastic Joyce's use of the *Odyssey* turns out to be, is sorely missing in *Finnegans Wake*. The whole book is a dream – but a dream purporting to contain the history of the world. Even more so than in *Ulysses*, then, we will have to abandon the habit of reading for the story. Again, this fact will not be without its critics. We cannot, though, say that Joyce didn't anticipate this:

> You is feeling like you was lost in the bush, boy? You says: It is a puling sample jungle of words. You most shouts out: Bethicket me for a stump of a beech if I have the poultriest notion what the farest he all means. [p. 112]

There are, however, two interesting models for such narrative strategies: one suggested by Joyce himself, the other by the Irish poet Paul Muldoon.

In 1922 Joyce sent Harriet Weaver a facsimile copy of the *Book of Kells*, the 8th-century illuminated book of the four New Testament gospels, and which he later claimed to have carried with him on all his travels. "It is," Joyce said, "the most purely Irish thing we have. Indeed, you can compare much of my work to the intricate Illuminations." The *Book of Kells* makes an appearance in *Finnegans Wake*, though even here Joyce is playing games and has his own novel predate and inspire it!

Muldoon's comments, though they tie in with the 'discursive' quality of Illuminated books and the ways in which decoration (or digressions and repetitions) appear for their own sake, are to do with what he calls "the valorisation of obliquity and tangentiality" that he sees as an important aspect of many Irish writers. These, Muldoon continues, coexist with two other phenomena: "the slip and slop of language, a disregard for the line between sense and nonsense", and "an almost total disregard for linear narrative [that stems from] the tradition of popular song and the street ballad."[6] With this in mind, we might best imagine *Finnegans Wake* (among other things) as a fusion of the intricate art of the *Book of Kells* and the popular ballad of Tim Finnegan – a hod-carrier who falls from his ladder and is presumed dead, only to be revived at his wake by the smell of whisky – the chorus of which contains plenty of Muldoon's slip and slop:

> Whack folthe dah, dance to your partner.
>   Welt the flure, yer trotters shake,
> Wasn't it the truth I told you,
>   Lots of fun at Finnegan's Wake.

I want, now, to develop this matter of language in the novel and the relation, as it were, of the parts to the whole. This is no easy matter. And while it cannot offer a shortcut through the thicket of *Finnegans Wake*, it might go some way to allaying the suspicion that the novel is a kind of high-modernist or postmodern practical joke at the reader's expense.

There are something in the order of 65 languages present in *Finnegans Wake*. Little wonder, then, that Joyce is held up as the

Cosmopolitan writer par excellence, and that his works have Universal significance. The first of these terms, however, is more useful than the latter, locating Joyce as it does in the urban and in that aspect of Modernism that relied on the experience of artists living and working in exile. And though the word didn't always carry positive associations – Jews, for example, were disparagingly thought of as being a dangerously 'Cosmopolitan' influence – it at least has the merit of focusing our attention on the woof and weave, or slip and slop of Joyce's word games and the ways in which he is, as Muldoon suggests, a quintessentially Irish writer. That this needs saying is perhaps surprising. Yet as Professor T.P. Dolan argued in a lecture given in Dublin in February 2003, Joyce's Irishness is under fire.[7]

Taking issue with the American scholar Morton P. Levitt, the author of *James Joyce and Modernism: Beyond Dublin*, Dolan argues that far from writing in a 'universal' or 'global' English, Joyce's source is Dublin and its "uniquely Irish version of English" – an English which, Dolan says, is "older than London English". Rather than being a remnant of some pre-modern era, however, Hiberno-English is, to cite *Finnegans Wake*, "as modern as tomorrow afternoon and in appearance up to the minute". In terms of Joyce's earlier writings, his use of Hiberno-English appears in particular details, an example of which is the famous scene in *A Portrait* when Stephen is talking to the English dean of studies:

> – What funnel? asked Stephen.
> – The funnel through which you pour oil into your lamp.
> – That? said Stephen. Is that called a funnel? Is it not a tundish?
> – What is a tundish?
> – That. The ... the funnel.
> – Is that called a tundish in Ireland? asked the dean. I never heard the word in my life.
> – It is called a tundish in Lower Drumcondra, said Stephen laughing, where they speak the best English.
> [*A Portrait,* pp. 203-4]

This shows the influence of Joyce's reading of the Italian philosopher Giovanni Battista Vico (1668-1744), who saw no essential difference between the study of language and the study of history. His great insight was that history isn't divinely inspired but of human origin and found in myths, languages, customs and events. "It follows," Vico wrote, "that the first science to be learned should be mythology or the interpretation of fables, which were the first histories of the gentile nations." Thus language is where we find evidence of the external world, both as it is perceived by the individual mind and as it has affected the development of nations and communities. Language, then, is the point at which the internal and external worlds meet: "just as the bodily eye sees all objects outside itself but needs a mirror to see itself." The implications of Vico's statement in terms of *Ulysses* and Stephen's "cracked lookingglass" cannot be overestimated. As was stated in the previous chapter, what Joyce wants is to draw our attention to the means by which things are represented. In *Finnegans Wake* this means nothing less than the wholesale reconstitution of the English language. For while a phrase such as "melumps and mumpos of the hoose uncommons" can be translated as "my lords and ladies of the House of Commons", to do so is only to find an equivalence for what Joyce wrote. The important thing to recognise is that the 'how' and 'what' of *Finnegans Wake* cannot so easily be pulled apart. 'Funnel' and 'tundish' may refer to the same object; in terms of what they signify, however, they are poles apart.

Dolan calls the tundish episode an example of "linguistic apartheid". This is a strong charge to make, until we see that language is being used to assert authority. The English dean is in no doubt which is the correct term, 'tundish' being merely an interesting local variation. Stephen is only too aware of this:

> How different are the words home, Christ, ale, master, on his lips than mine! I cannot speak or write these words without unrest of spirit ... My soul frets in the shadow of his language.
> [*A Portrait*, p. 205]

Finnegans Wake, then, is the other side of this fretfulness – of the silence and cunning adopted by Stephen. "Here form *is* content, content *is* form," Samuel Beckett wrote in his contribution to *Our Exagmination Round His Factification for Incamination of Work in Progress*. "[Joyce's] writing is not *about* something; *it is that something itself*." And that something, as the Irish Beckett knew only too well, is what that the King's or Queen's English was incapable of saying, or thought politic to keep mum about:

> Mr Joyce has desophisticated language. And it is worth while remarking that no language is so sophisticated as English. It is abstracted to death ... This writing that you find so obscure is a quintessential extraction of language and painting and gesture[.] Here is the savage economy of hieroglyphics. Here words are not the polite contortions of 20th century printer's ink. They are alive.

I doubt that there's a better description of the deadening effects of Standard English than Beckett's "polite contortions". To me it brings to mind Stanley Spencer's wonderful painting *Christ Preaching at Cookham Regatta: Dinner on the Hotel Lawn*, in which he shows the arms and wrists of the servants who are laying the tables for the dressed-to-the-nines gentry contorted into unnatural gestures that exemplify the rituals of class. What Joyce ultimately rejected, Beckett says, is the idea that "language was nothing but a polite and conventional symbolism".

The point remains to be made, however, that Joyce's use of grammar, syntax and language in *Finnegans Wake* cannot be narrowly understood as simply replacing Standard English with Hiberno-English. The novel ranges much further afield than this in its linguistic concerns. In doing so it reflects an essential aspect of both Joyce's personal circumstances and a vital phenomena of the modern world: the experience of being a refugee, exile or émigré. This has been commented on by Amin Maalouf, and what he says (though it may require certain readjustments of thinking or an imaginative leap on the part of those who are native English-speakers or who have grown up during the phenomenal technological changes of the last two decades or so) allows us a way into *Finnegans Wake* that we might otherwise miss, while also enlightening us on the novel's essential hybridity:

> Isn't it a characteristic of the age we live in that it has made everyone in a way a migrant and a member of a minority? We all have to live in a universe bearing little resemblance to the place where we were born: we must all learn other languages, other modes of speech, other codes; and we all have the feeling

that our identity, as we have conceived of it since we were children, is threatened.

While there are positive features to this condition of delight at the variousness of the state of things, there are also implicit dangers. These too cannot be expunged from our reading of *Finnegans Wake*, and have been defined by Maalouf as the "danger of pique and resentment" that counters the omnipotence of hegemony. What Maalouf means by this is that there are many who remain "so angry or bewildered that they give up trying to understand what is going on ... They huddle themselves away, they barricade themselves in, they close their minds, they ruminate, they give up looking for anything new, they are afraid of the future, of the present and of everyone else." Such, anyway, will it seem to many readers are the effects of Joyce's deliberate evasions and rejections of the English language. By the same token there are aspects of *Finnegans Wake* that can also be read as a direct challenging of the hegomonic claims and national aspirations of the new Irish Republic as laid out in the Constitution of 1937, which made a number of assumptions about the nature and identity of Ireland: that it was Catholic, and that the Roman Catholic Church be granted "a special position ... as the guardian of the faith professed by the great majority of the citizens"; that divorce should be illegal; that working mothers should be denounced (Articles 40, 41 and 45 implied or declared that a woman's place was in the home); that a high priority was placed on the restoration of the Irish language and culture (Tomás Derrig, the Minister of Education, asserted in 1943 the necessity of "waging a most intense war against English, and against human nature itself, for the life of the language."). The novel, then, can be seen as cutting Joyce adrift from both the old and new Ireland, as it does from English as it is anywhere spoken.

Beckett's "form *is* content, content *is* form" alerts us to another aspect of language, one which returns us to Joyce's concern with interrogating the workings of discourse and ideology. I have commented on how Joyce brings into doubt the validity of various cultural myths, and the series of binary oppositions that underpin them. This process, described by Karen Lawrence as "a radical questioning of the notion of origin" is not without its contradictions. If we think of the representation of the Catholic Church in the stories and novels there can be little question that Joyce is openly hostile; yet a great deal of the emotional power of Joyce's writing can rely on moments when the symbolism of Catholicism is made use of. Think of Rudy's appearance at the end of 'Circe'. What I am suggesting, then, is that Joyce's critique of various institutions often takes place not from *without* but from *within* them. The implication being that no one can step wholly outside discourse or ideology. The aim of the artist, to return briefly to the theories of Walter Benjamin, is to search out those fragments of experience that are capable of being used to read history against the grain. Hence the centrality of the epiphany.

In terms of *Finnegans Wake*, a book which looks to expose how we come to censor and repress certain instinctual aspects of our selves, Joyce realised that he needed a 'dream' language if he was to accurately write of, and from, the unconscious. The form and content of the book are therefore indissoluble. Trying to translate *Finnegans Wake* into Standard English is analogous to telling someone the details of a particularly complex dream. The more we try to rationalise and structure the dream, the more we try to turn it from symbol and metaphor into narrative, the more the lived experience of the dream slips through the spaces between words. Dreams, as Jung tells us, have a structure unlike that of the other contents of consciousness. In terms of the history of the novel, the same is true of *Finnegans Wake*. Similarly, what Jung has further to say about dreams is also true of the experience of reading (or failing to read) *Finnegans Wake*:

> The combination of ideas in dreams is essentially fantastic; they are linked together in a sequence which is as a rule quite foreign to our 'reality thinking', and in striking contrast to the logical sequence of ideas which we consider to be a special characteristic of conscious mental processes.[8]

The big difference between Jung and *Finnegans Wake*, of course, is that Jung is writing *about* dreams and he is making use of "reality thinking". Joyce, however, is not writing *about* dreams; the novel *is* a dream, or rather a vast number of dreams. To accede to "reality thinking" would mean handing over the novel to the censor. In a very real sense, then, the meaning of the novel is beyond its author's control. Or as the French symbolist poet Rimbaud put it: "The expression of these concepts can be achieved only through the rhythmic 'hallucination of the word'".

This chapter began with the suggestion that *Finnegans Wake* wanted to demolish the "assured place" of its author in western culture. That Joyce wanted to do this is implicated in the fact that, as Seamus Deane says, "Anything and everything could go into the *Wake*. Many of its local 'meanings' are randomly generated". Authority and authorial control, then, lie with language and not the individual writer. In this way Joyce hoped to free language, the author and the reader from the responsibility of meaning as opposed to being. In this he shares an aspect of Wittgenstein's approach to philosophy: that it should be an activity and not a set of prescriptive laws, and that its aim should be the clarification of the limits of meaningful language. In more ways than one, *Finnegans Wake* pushes such 'meaningful language' about as far as we can imagine. It also, of course, forces us to reconsider what might be meant by meaningful *reading*.

In his essay 'The Task of the Translator', Walter Benjamin provocatively declared that "No poem is intended for the reader, no picture for the beholder, no symphony for the listener."[9] What Benjamin is asking his reader to consider (and we can assume that the essay is intended for 'no reader') is that any work of art is immediately limited in its scope by having a prescribed meaning imposed on it at its inception. This isn't a defence of elitism; simply a statement of what to the truly democratic artist is a matter of belief: that art is an activity and a process rather than a product. Likewise *Finnegans Wake* was clearly meant for 'no reader', or rather for 'no two readers'. The novel is in excess of whatever individual reading we take from it. It challenges what is meant by, in John Lucas' resonant phrase, the "imaginatively viable". In this it would seem to insist on reading as a collective or communal activity. Which returns us to another aspect of what Beckett had to say about the book, a comment which more than ever makes *Finnegans Wake* sound like the *Book of Kells*:

> You complain that this stuff is not written in English. It is not written at all. It is not to be read – or rather it is not only to be read. *It is to be looked at and listened to* [my italics].

Beckett has been taken at his word. In February 2003 the James Joyce Institute of Ireland finished its group reading of *Finnegans Wake*, a reading that took place at weekly intervals which began in September 1995. Derek Attridge has written usefully about such a process, and how it can counter some of the seemingly insurmountable problems the novel sets the individual reader: "Each member of the group contributes his or her particular insights, which in turn trigger others, in a process which creates a growing network of meanings and patterns". The further merits of such a process, Attridge says, is that they draw attention to the fact that the novel cannot be mastered:

> All reading, the *Wake* insists, is an endless interchange: the reader is affected by the text at the same time as the text is affected by the reader, and neither retains a secure identity upon which the other can depend.[10]

If this sounds a hopelessly romantic notion of the Republic of Letters, we might want to think about how much it actually parallels the process by which Joyce came to write *Finnegans Wake*.

Even after completion, *Ulysses* continued to exert enormous influence over Joyce. In particular it was the character of Molly Bloom which remained restless, refusing to lie still in bed. This is clear from differing accounts of the same dream that Joyce had about Molly appearing and reproaching him for having written 'Penelope'. In one version Joyce recounts how Molly asked him "What are you meddling with my old business for?" She appeared carrying a coffin, and said "If you don't change this is for you." The dream sheds interesting light on Molly's disquiet at the attempts of male authors to represent female characters, and reminds us that in 1916 Joyce had kept a notebook in which he recorded Nora's dreams alongside his own interpretation of them. Furthermore, the coffin and her threat to put Joyce inside it puts us in mind of Tim Finnegan, and our anxiety as to whether he is dead or simply unconscious after suffering his fall. What is clear, though, is that *Ulysses* continued to affect Joyce. Might we go further and say that *Finnegans Wake* was written in response to, or a reaction against its predecessor; that the later novel is part of an "endless interchange" between Joyce the writer and Joyce the reader? *Finnegans Wake* seems to suggest as much, never more so than when Anna Livia Plurabelle comments on the implications of Joyce having written 'Penelope':

> the fatal droopadwindle slope of the blamed scawl, a sure sign of imperfectible moral blindness, the toomuchness, the fartoomanyness … sternly controlled and easily repursuaded by the uniform matteroffactness of a meandering male fist[.]

This suggests that Joyce came to fear that *Ulysses* was itself an act of colonialism, with the male author appropriating female consciousness. That *Finnegans Wake* sought to undo this damage is strongly argued by Karen Lawrence when she says that while Molly "represents the *problem of woman represented by the male pen*, a staging of alterity that reveals itself as masquerade". *Finnegans Wake* – and in particular Anna Livia Plurabelle – shows that for the male writer the female must always remain "elusive, a desire that can never be possessed." Anna Livia Plurabelle is the female personified. Her medium is water. Hence the slippery-sloppiness of the text. What Joyce articulates through her, then, is his faith that character and language must be allowed to go beyond themselves.

In a diary entry written a month after their mother's death, Stanislaus Joyce wrote the following astute comments about his brother:

> Jim is thought to be very frank about himself but his style is such that it might be contended that he confesses in a foreign language – an easier confession than in the vulgar tongue.

Though *Finnegans Wake* is the apotheosis of Joyce's confessional style, and the demands it makes on readers to 'translate' it, nevertheless its achievements, unique as they are, are built on the strongest foundations. From the italicised aura surrounding the words *"paralysis"*, *"gnomon"* and *"simony"* in the opening sentences of *Dubliners*, Joyce insists on our coming to terms with, in Walter Benjamin's words, "the foreignness of language." By this Benjamin means that whatever and whenever we write we are, as it were, translating our experiences into something other. In doing so, as with the use Joyce made of his epiphanies, "the original [experience] rises into a higher and purer linguistic air". That this can only ever be provisional state shouldn't deter us. Benjamin continues:

> It cannot live there permanently, to be sure, and it certainly does not reach it in its entirety. Yet, in a singularly impressive manner, at least it points the way to this region: the predestined, hitherto inaccessible realm of reconciliation and fulfilment of languages.

And while Stephen walks into eternity along Sandymount Strand, Bloom asserts that all languages must be seen as versions of the local and familiar:

> It's all very fine to boast of mutual superiority but what about mutual equality? I resent violence or intolerance in any shape or form. It never reaches anything or stops anything. A revolution must come on the due instalments plan. It's a patent absurdity on the face of it to hate people because they live round the corner and speak another vernacular, so to speak.

The astuteness of Stanislaus' analysis also applies to the word 'confession'. Throughout *A Portrait*, for example, we witness Stephen making a whole variety of confessions: to his schoolmates regarding whether he kisses his mother before going to bed, and to the prefect of studies regarding his broken glasses; to Heron and a group of other students regarding his favourite authors, and to the nationalist Cranly regarding his lack of faith in the idea of nation. Above all, there is his scared-out-of-his-wits confession to a Catholic priest regarding his visits to prostitutes. Stephen's confessions, then, define him as a character. It is a form of discourse written about by Foucault, who called it "a ritual … in which the speaking subject is also the subject of the statement". This is clearly important in terms of Joyce's writing, providing as it does a summary of the struggle of all his characters to inherit language and inhabit their own lives.

Foucault's critique of the discourse of confession and its relation to sex has other parallels with Joyce's fiction, not least the auto-biographical aspects of his work and the authority Joyce's (re)authorised version of events bestows on the fictional lives of his characters. Confession, Foucault writes:

lends itself, if not to other domains, at least to new ways of exploring the existing ones. It is no longer a question simply of saying what was done ... and how it was done; but of reconstructing, in and around the act, the thoughts that recapitulated it, the obsessions that accompanied it, the images, desires, modulations, and quality of the pleasure that animated it.

What Foucault is advocating is confession as a socially legislated discourse, a discourse that looks beyond individual actions and at the whole culture of feelings that surround it. What must strike us as extraordinary in Joyce is the unsparing nature and quality of his confession and how, in Foucault's terms, it becomes "an obligatory act of speech which, under some imperious compulsion, breaks the bonds of discretion or forgetfulness." Joyce's "obligatory act" leaves us all in his debt.

Footnotes

[1] 'Hauteur', *London Review of Books* (23 May 2003), pp. 10-12.

[2] 'Joyce and Feminism', *The Cambridge Companion to James Joyce*, pp. 237-258.

[3] 'The First Person', *The Wittgenstein Reader*, edited Anthony Kenny (Oxford: Blackwell, 1994), pp. 191-207.

[4] 'Sexual Linguistics; gender, language, sexuality', *New Literary History* 16 (1985), pp. 515-43.

[5] 'Finnegans Wake', *Cambridge Companion to James Joyce*, 161-184.

[6] *To Ireland, I: The Clarendon Lectures in English Literature 1998* (Oxford University Press: Oxford, 2000).

[7] A condensed version of Professor Dolan's 'Joyce Perspectives' lecture was published by the James Joyce Centre in the 2003 *James Joyce Bloomsday Magazine*, pp. 35-37.

[8] 'General Aspects of Dream Psychology' (1948), *Dreams* (Routledge Classics: London, 2002).

[9] *Illuminations* (Fontana Press: London, 1992), 70-82.

[10] 'Reading Joyce', *The Cambridge Companion to James Joyce*, 1-30.

Select Bibliography

Editions

Critical and scholarly debate surrounding the texts of Joyce's writings are as involved as commentaries on the books themselves. I have taken my quotations from the Penguin editions of *Dubliners*, *A Portrait of the Artist as a Young Man,* and *Finnegans Wake*. All quotations from *Ulysses*, meanwhile, are from The Bodley Head edition, edited by Hans Walter Gabler.

Dubliners, with an Introduction and Notes by Terence Brown (Penguin: Harmondsworth, 1992).

Dubliners, with an Introduction and Notes by Jeri Johnson (Oxford University Press: Oxford, 2000).

A Portrait of the Artist as a Young Man, edited with an Introduction and Notes by Seamus Deane (Penguin: Harmondsworth, 1992).

A Portrait of the Artist as a Young Man, edited with an Introduction and Notes by Jeri Johnson (Oxford University Press: Oxford, 2000).

Ulysses (The 1922 text), edited with an Introduction and Notes by Jeri Johnson (Oxford University Press: Oxford, 1998).

Ulysses, edited by Hans Walter Gabler with Wolfhard Steppe and Claus Melchior, Afterword by Michael Groden (The Bodley Head: London, 1993).

Finnegans Wake, with an Introduction by Seamus Deane (Penguin: Harmondsworth, 1992).

Poems and Shorter Writings, edited by Richard Ellmann, A. Walton Litz and John Whittier-Ferguson (Faber and Faber: London, 1991).

Poems and Exiles, edited by J.C.C. Mays (Penguin: Harmondsworth, 1992).

Stephen Hero, edited with an Introduction by Theodor Spencer, revised edition with additional material and Forword by John J. Slocum and Herbert Cahoon (Cape: London, 1956).

Occasional, Critical, and Political Writing, edited with an Introduction and Notes by Kevin Barry (Oxford University Press: Oxford, 2000).

Selected Letters of James Joyce, edited by Richard Ellmann (New York: Viking, 1975).

Critical

Attridge, Derek, (ed.) *The Cambridge Companion to James Joyce* (Cambridge University Press: Cambridge, 1990).

Beckett, Samuel, *et al.*, *Our Exagmination Round His Factification for Incamination of Work in Progress* (1929), (Faber and Faber: London, 1972).

Bloom, Harold, (ed.) *Modern Critical Views: James Joyce* (Chelsea House Publishers: New York, 1986).

Bolt, Sydney, *A Preface to James Joyce* (Longman: London and New York, 1981).

Budgen, Frank, *James Joyce and the Making of 'Ulysses'* (1934) (Oxford University Press: Oxford, 1972).

Burgess, Anthony, *Here Comes Everybody: An Introduction to James Joyce for the Ordinary Reader* (Faber and Faber: London, 1965).

Cheng, Vincent J., *Joyce, Race, And Empire* (Cambridge University Press: Cambridge, 1995).

Connor, Stephen, *James Joyce* (Northcote House in association with The British Council: London, 1996).

Deming, Robert H. (ed.) *James Joyce: the Critical Heritage*, Vols. I & II (Routledge & Kegan Paul Limited: London, 1970).

Ellmann, Richard, *Ulysses on the Liffey* (Faber and Faber: London, 1974).

Gross, John, *Joyce* (3rd Impression with corrections) (Fontana: London, 1976).

Kenner, Hugh, *Dublin's Joyce* (1956) (Columbia University Press: New York, 1987).

Levin, Harry, *James Joyce: A Critical Introduction* (1941) Revised edition (New Directions Press: New York, 1960).

McHugh, Roland, *Annotations to Finnegans Wake* (Routledge: London, 1980).

Wilson, Edmund, 'James Joyce', *Axel's Castle: A Study of the Imaginative Literature of 1870-1930* (1931) (The Modern Library: New York, 1996).

Biographical

Ellman, Richard, *James Joyce*, New and Revised Edition (Oxford University Press: Oxford, 1982).

Joyce, Stanislaus, *My Brother's Keeper: James Joyce's Early Years* (ed.) Richard Ellmann (Faber and Faber: London, 1958).

Maddox, Brenda, *Nora: A Biography of Nora Joyce* (Hamish Hamilton: London, 1988).

GREENWICH EXCHANGE BOOKS

Greenwich Exchange Student Guides are critical studies of major or contemporary serious writers in English and selected European languages. The series is for the student, the teacher and 'common readers' and is an ideal resource for libraries. The *Times Educational Supplement* praised these books, saying, "The style of these guides has a pressure of meaning behind it. Students should learn from that ... If art is about selection, perception and taste, then this is it."

(ISBN prefix 1-871551- applies)
The series includes:
W.H. Auden by Stephen Wade (36-6)
Honoré de Balzac by Wendy Mercer (48-X)
William Blake hy Peter Davies (27-7)
The Brontës by Peter Davies (24-2)
Robert Browning by John Lucas (59-5)
Samuel Taylor Coleridge by Andrew Keanie (64-1)
Joseph Conrad by Martin Seymour-Smith (18-8)
William Cowper by Michael Thorn (25-0)
Charles Dickens by Robert Giddings (26-9)
Emily Dickinson by Marnie Pomeroy (68-4)
John Donne by Sean Haldane (23-4)
Robert Frost by Warren Hope (70-6)
Ford Madox Ford by Anthony Fowles (63-3)
Thomas Hardy by Sean Haldane (35-1)
Seamus Heaney by Warren Hope (37-4)
Philip Larkin by Warren Hope (35-8)
Laughter in the Dark – The Plays of Joe Orton by Arthur Burke (56-0)
Philip Roth by Paul McDonald (72-2)
Shakespeare's Non-Dramatic Poetry by Martin Seymour-Smith (22-6)
Shakespeare's Othello by Matt Simpson (71-4)
Shakespeare's Sonnets by Martin Seymour-Smith (38-2)
Tobias Smollett by Robert Giddings (21-8)
Alfred, Lord Tennyson by Michael Thorn (20-X)
William Wordsworth by Andrew Keanie (57-9)

OTHER GREENWICH EXCHANGE BOOKS

Paperback unless otherwise stated.

Shakespeare's Sonnets

Martin Seymour-Smith

Martin Seymour-Smith's outstanding achievement lies in the field of literary biography and criticism. In 1963 he produced his comprehensive edition, in the old spelling, of *Shakespeare's Sonnets* (here revised and corrected by himself and Peter Davies in 1998). With its landmark introduction and its brilliant critical commentary on each sonnet, it was praised by William Empson and John Dover Wilson. Stephen Spender said of him "I greatly admire Martin Seymour-Smith for the independence of his views and the great interest of his mind"; and both Robert Graves and Anthony Burgess described him as the leading critic of his time. His exegesis of the *Sonnets* remains unsurpassed.

2001 • 194 pages • ISBN 1-871551-38-2

English Language Skills

Vera Hughes

If you want to be sure, (as a student, or in your business or personal life,) that your written English is correct, this book is for you. Vera Hughes' aim is to help you remember the basic rules of spelling, grammar and punctuation. 'Noun', 'verb', 'subject', 'object' and 'adjective' are the only technical terms used. The book teaches the clear, accurate English required by the business and office world. It coaches acceptable current usage and makes the rules easier to remember.

Vera Hughes was a civil servant and is a trainer and author of training manuals.

2002 • 142 pages • ISBN 1-871551-60-9

LITERARY CRITICISM

The Author, the Book and the Reader

Robert Giddings

This collection of essays analyses the effects of changing technology and the attendant commercial pressures on literary styles and subject matter. Authors covered include Charles Dickens, Tobias George Smollett, Mark Twain, Dr Johnson and John le Carré.

1991 • 220 pages • illustrated • ISBN 1-871551-01-3

Liar! Liar!: Jack Kerouac – Novelist
R.J. Ellis

The fullest study of Jack Kerouac's fiction to date. It is the first book to devote an individual chapter to every one of his novels. *On the Road*, *Visions of Cody* and *The Subterraneans* are reread in-depth, in a new and exciting way. *Visions of Gerard* and *Doctor Sax* are also strikingly reinterpreted, as are other daringly innovative writings, like 'The Railroad Earth' and his "try at a spontaneous *Finnegan's Wake*" – *Old Angel Midnight*. Neglected writings, such as *Tristessa* and *Big Sur*, are also analysed, alongside better-known novels such as *Dharma Bums* and *Desolation Angels*.

R.J. Ellis is Senior Lecturer in English at Nottingham Trent University.

1999 • 295 pages • ISBN 1-871551-53-6

BIOGRAPHY

The Good That We Do
John Lucas

John Lucas' book blends fiction, biography and social history in order to tell the story of his grandfather, Horace Kelly. Headteacher of a succession of elementary schools in impoverished areas of London, 'Hod' Kelly was also a keen cricketer, a devotee of the music hall, and included among his friends the great Trade Union leader, Ernest Bevin. In telling the story of his life, Lucas has provided a fascinating range of insights into the lives of ordinary Londoners from the First World War until the outbreak of the Second World War. Threaded throughout is an account of such people's hunger for education, and of the different ways government, church and educational officialdom ministered to that hunger. *The Good That We Do* is both a study of one man and of a period when England changed, drastically and forever.

John Lucas is Professor of English at Nottingham Trent University and is a poet and critic.

2001 • 214 pages • ISBN 1-871551-54-4

In Pursuit of Lewis Carroll
Raphael Shaberman

Sherlock Holmes and the author uncover new evidence in their investigations into the mysterious life and writing of Lewis Carroll. They examine published works by Carroll that have been overlooked by previous commentators. A newly discovered poem, almost certainly by Carroll, is published here.

Amongst many aspects of Carroll's highly complex personality, this book explores his relationship with his parents, numerous child friends, and the formidable Mrs Liddell, mother of the immortal Alice. Raphael Shaberman

was a founder member of the Lewis Carroll Society and a teacher of autistic children.
1994 • 118 pages • illustrated • ISBN 1-871551-13-7

Musical Offering
Yolanthe Leigh
In a series of vivid sketches, anecdotes and reflections, Yolanthe Leigh tells the story of her growing up in the Poland of the 1930s and the Second World War. These are poignant episodes of a child's first encounters with both the enchantments and the cruelties of the world; and from a later time, stark memories of the brutality of the Nazi invasion, and the hardships of student life in Warsaw under the Occupation. But most of all this is a record of inward development; passages of remarkable intensity and simplicity describe the girl's response to religion, to music, and to her discovery of philosophy.
Yolanthe Leigh was formerly a Lecturer in Philosophy at Reading University.
2000 • 57 pages • ISBN: 1-871551-46-3

Norman Cameron
Warren Hope
Norman Cameron's poetry was admired by W.H. Auden, celebrated by Dylan Thomas and valued by Robert Graves. He was described by Martin Seymour-Smith as, "one of … the most rewarding and pure poets of his generation …" and is at last given a full length biography. This eminently sociable man, who had periods of darkness and despair, wrote little poetry by comparison with others of his time, but always of a consistently high quality – imaginative and profound.
2000 • 221 pages • illustrated • ISBN 1-871551-05-6

POETRY

Adam's Thoughts in Winter
Warren Hope
Warren Hope's poems have appeared from time to time in a number of literary periodicals, pamphlets and anthologies on both sides of the Atlantic. They appeal to lovers of poetry everywhere. His poems are brief, clear, frequently lyrical, characterised by wit, but often distinguished by tenderness. The poems gathered in this first book-length collection counter the brutalising ethos of contemporary life, speaking of and for the virtues of modesty, honesty and gentleness in an individual, memorable way.
2000 • 47 pages • ISBN 1-871551-40-4

Baudelaire: Les Fleurs du Mal
Translated by F.W. Leakey
Selected poems from *Les Fleurs du Mal* are translated with parallel French texts and are designed to be read with pleasure by readers who have no French as well as those who are practised in the French language.
F.W. Leakey was Professor of French in the University of London. As a scholar, critic and teacher he specialised in the work of Baudelaire for 50 years and published a number of books on the poet.
2001 • 153 pages • ISBN 1-871551-10-2

Lines from the Stone Age
Sean Haldane
Reviewing Sean Haldane's 1992 volume *Desire in Belfast*, Robert Nye wrote in *The Times* that "Haldane can be sure of his place among the English poets." This place is not yet a conspicuous one, mainly because his early volumes appeared in Canada and because he has earned his living by other means than literature. Despite this, his poems have always had their circle of readers. The 60 previously unpublished poems of *Lines from the Stone Age* – "lines of longing, terror, pride, lust and pain" – may widen this circle.
2000 • 53 pages • ISBN 1-871551-39-0

Wilderness
Martin Seymour-Smith
This is Martin Seymour-Smith's first publication of his poetry for more than twenty years. This collection of 36 poems is a fearless account of an inner life of love, frustration, guilt, laughter and the celebration of others. He is best known to the general public as the author of the controversial and bestselling *Hardy* (1994).
1994 • 52 pages • ISBN 1-871551-08-0